The First Ten Days

Robert W. Haeussinger

June 2013, Sept 2019

TABLE OF CONTENTS

Day One – Pre Dawn, *Blair House* 5

Day One 10

Day Two 25

Day Three 32

Day Four 49

Day Five 80

Day Six 114

Day 7 164

Day 8 188

Day 9 210

Day 10 255

Sunday, March 10 4:30 am 287

Mr. Vice President, yes; sir the President is dead.

Day One – Pre Dawn, *Blair House*
Thursday, February 29 3:15 am

"Mr. Vice President, please wake up."

"Ben I'm awake, did I hear you say the President was dead."

"Yes Mr. Keller you did."

"Ben, how did it happen?"

"Sir, the First Lady found him unconscious, stretched out on the couch in the Presidential library. The President typically goes to the library after supper to read reports and draft correspondence. When the President didn't come to bed, the First Lady went looking for him. She repeatedly tried to wake him, but could not. It was she called Doctor Boardman, the President's physician. Doctor Boardman immediately examined the President and found him not breathing and a faint pulse, then that stopped. The Doctor pronounced the President dead at 2:52 am."

"Ben does Boardman know what from or why?"

"No sir, there were no obvious signs."

"Mr. Vice President, you must get dressed and come with me. I already called The Chief Justice, the Cabinet and Congressional Leaders; they'll join you in the East Room for your swearing in."

Look at me, I'm a mess. This is not a good way to start the day. How can the President be dead, I had lunch with him two days ago, he seemed fine and in good spirit? First, I lost my wife to a drunk driver, now my best friend, the President, both dead.

It seemed like only yesterday he called to tell me the Vice President had resigned, due to poor health, and would I accept nomination as his replacement. That was last July. Now I'm replacing the President, it doesn't seem right. Now all I can do is stare out the window, and think about what lies ahead; I feel like I could throw up. I should talk to someone, but everyone is in bed. Maybe a shower will help me relax.

As the water runs down my back, I start to recall how I got into politics. As Chairman of the City Planning Commission, the Mayor and I were always clashing. He had his way I had mine. The group that later recruited me, as a write-in candidate for mayor, thought I was right and the Mayor wrong. The voters thought so to; and now I am about to become President of the United States. As I finish my shower, I realized I hadn't lathered up, the soap dish is empty.

Now what suit should I wear, my favorite, the blue one, or the black one. I hate black it reminds me of a funeral parlor. When I finish dressing, I'll ask Anders how I look.

"Anders, how do I look?"

"Mr. Vice President, your tie doesn't match your suit, and your shoes are untied."

"Sorry Ben I guess my mind is elsewhere. Could you pick out a tie for me?"

"Sir, here's one that looks good, and by the way, you might want to comb your hair."

"Ben everything is happening so fast."

"Sir you're right, and I understand, it's perfectly natural to feel nervous"

"Ben, thanks for the encouragement, let's go."

As we walk to the East Room, I realize I have to make a brief statement after I'm sworn in. It should be in my own words. Let me think about that. Today I assume this office with a heavy heart. At 2:52 this morning our President, Andrew Leonard passed away. My sympathies go out to his family. As is the custom, President Leonard's body will lie in state in the Capitol rotunda, to allow citizens the opportunity to pay their respects. The good book tells us, out of tragedy comes renewal; faith shall get us through this difficult period. On a personal note, I take this office under the most difficult of circumstances. Therefore, I ask for your help in the days ahead. Maybe I best write it down, so I won't forget it. Now time to talk to the First Lady.

I admit, I don't know her very well, even though the President and I were close friends. As a courtesy to her, I'm going ask the First Lady for permission for an autopsy. Given the mysterious nature of the President's death, an autopsy is vital. Something tells me all is not right; a healthy man in his mid fifties doesn't up and die. If foul play is involved, we must find out who is responsible.

"Ben could you let Mrs. Leonard know I need to speak to her as soon as possible."

"Mrs. Leonard, I need to speak with you privately. Sue, with your permission I must order an autopsy on the President. If anything is found out of the ordinary, we'll not release the results, and conduct a thorough investigation into his death. Do I have your approval?"

"Yes Mr. President, you do"

"Thank you."

"I have to go now; the Chief Justice is waiting to swear me in."

Day One

Thursday, February 29 4:30am

"Mr. Chief Justice, we best do this"

"Anders, please hand me the Bible I brought along."

"Mr. President, are you ready to take the Oath?"

"Yes sir, I'm ready"

"Mr. President, repeat after me, I..."

"I John August Keller do solemnly swear that I will faithfully execute the Office of President of the United States, and will to the best of my ability, preserve, protect and defend the Constitution of the United States, so help me God..."

"Congratulations Mr. President."

"Thank you, Mr. Chief Justice. Anders, please ask the White House staff and the Cabinet to meet me in the Oval Office in ten minutes. Mr. Attorney General, let's take a walk. Sir, I'm ordering an immediate autopsy of the President; I've communicated my intention to the First Lady, and she has no objections. Until we know the results, the findings shall remain private."

"Mr. President, I'll prepare the paperwork."

I admit, I hardly know the Attorney General, but for now, I have to trust him to do as I ask.
Perhaps I should call Lynn, my sister-in-law, the doctor, and ask her to assist with the autopsy. She can be my quality assurance specialist; her specialty, pathology. At least I can count on one honest answer on the team. For now, that can wait.

11

I now find myself alone, saddled with the enormous duties of President of the Unites States. I will need to prove to the American people that I'm up to the task. Some people are already starting to question my ability, but that's Washington for you; enough whining time to get started. First stop, a visit with the Presidential staff. They are waiting in the Cabinet Room.

"Ladies and gentlemen let me begin by saying, all of us experienced a tremendous loss this morning and grieve we must. We also have to carry on. It's now my job to lead the country, but I need your help to do it. Since I've only been in Washington a short time, we've had little chance to work together. I know some of you might have concerns about that. If any wish to leave, I won't stand in your way."

"The next few days will be difficult for all of us, especially me. For now, I'm going to ask the Vice President's staff to work with you to address immediate concerns. Hopefully in a couple weeks, I will make the permanent assignments. Mr. Rogers, Wayne, any comments?"

"Mr. President, as Chief of Staff, I can assure you my immediate staff will do their job, and will support you completely."

"That's good to hear, now let's go to work. Mrs. Witt, stay, I need to talk to you privately."

Mrs. Witt, President Leonard always spoke highly of you. I know the two of you worked together for a long time. Would you consider working for me?

"Mr. President, the late President would expect me to, and I want to."

"Mrs. Witt, thank you. Oh before you go, a couple more things. Could you contact the Speaker of the House, the Senate Majority Leader, and Chair of the Joint Chiefs, and set appointments for each of them. Schedule the first one for nine o'clock, and the next two for 9:45 and 10:30 respectively. Also, call my sister-in-law Lynn and get her on the line."

Time will tell if keeping Mrs. Witt and Mr. Rogers onboard was a good decision. Something about that mousy Rogers concerns me I just can put my finger on it. Mrs. Witt can be a gossip when it suits her purpose. Generally gossips cannot be trusted, especially when it comes to sensitive information. She reminds me of my High School Librarian.

Now that I'm alone in the stately Cabinet Room, I should rethink my steps so far. Should I take a vigorous and unyielding approach or a more conciliatory course in conducting the country's affairs? There is so much to learn and so much to do, its mind boggling. The stillness, deafening, then the phone, its Lynn, my sister-in-law the doctor.

"Lynn it's nice to hear your voice."

"John when I got up this morning, I heard the news that the President was dead. I'm so sorry. How are you holding up, are you alright?"

"I'm okay, but I need to ask you a favor. Can you come to Washington and be my quality assurance specialist on the autopsy team? I need you to come now, today. The team will have just one day to exam the President's body. On Saturday, he'll lie in state at the Capitol Rotunda. Can you come?"

"Mr. President, John, I'm not sure I will have to clear it with my boss. You know he can be a pain when he wants to be, and that's most of the time. Can you find someone else?"

"No not really. I know now might not be a good time, but Lynn I really need your help. Do you want me to speak to your boss?"

"No John, that's not necessary. I suppose I can come, if you really need me."

"Lynn, I do. Please write this phone number down, it's my cell. 507-299-3333. Call me when you have your flight information, I'll have someone pick you up at the airport. You will be reimbursed for your expenses. I'll see you later, and thanks for coming."

Lynn is single and in her early forties, and is quite attractive. From the time we met, there's always been a subliminal friction between us. Maybe it's my fault. I thought her arrogant and rather high and mighty. As for her, she must speak for herself. As a professional, I respect her a great deal. She is an outstanding physician. She won't let the other physicians on the autopsy team push her around. I need an unbiased opinion, and she can provide it. If foul play was involved in the President's death, she would be the one to know of it.

"Mr. President."

"What is it Mrs. Witt?"

"Mr. President, Speaker Campbell is on the phone and insists on talking to you, personally."

The Speaker, in my view is a bull, always snorting and strutting in a lame attempt to get people to agree with him. True, I don't really know him, but that doesn't change my impression of him.

"Mr. Speaker, President Keller, what can I do for you sir?"

"Mr. Keller."

"It's President Keller."

My uncle taught me; grab the bull by the horn, so he won't gore you.

"Mr. President what are you going to do about the tax bill and what about health care."

It's clear, the Speaker is trying to rattle my cage; maybe he thinks he should be President.

"Calm down Mr. Speaker, there's plenty of time for that after the funeral and things calm a bit. I've studied the House and Senate versions of the tax bill, so I'm very familiar with the issues as they now stand. Before he died, President Leonard and I discussed the issues at length."

It's not what the Speaker wishes to hear; he and the President have their share of differences.

"Sir, Mrs. Witt will gladly schedule a time for us to meet so we can discuss the issues."

"Okay Mr. President."

"Good day Mr. Speaker."

One roadblock diverted, more ahead. My enemies and some of my fair weather friends will soon learn I'm no babe in the woods. Trust, but verify, and always follow up.

"Mrs. Witt could you ask my intern, Bernie Wagner, to come to my office."

"Bernie, I need you to check out a car and pick up my sister-in-law at the airport, she'll be landing at Reagan in about forty-five minutes; here's her flight information. Please bring her straight here; you're cleared to enter through the south gate. Do you have any questions?"

"No sir." *Bernie will not attract attention. I don't need any of that now.*

"Mrs. Witt, get the Attorney General on the phone."
"Mr. Attorney General, can you come to my office at 4:30 I want to discuss the autopsy."

"You can, see you then."

"Mrs. Witt, check if Mrs. Leonard is in the building; if she is, ask her to call me."

"Sue, John Keller, I hate to bother you on such short notice, but could you and Dr. Boardman come to my office in the West Wing at 4:30. You can, see you then, and Sue, use the private entrance, I'll explain later."

Lynn should be here a few minutes before the First Land and the Attorney General arrive.

"Thank you all for coming. Let me introduce my sister-in-law Lynn she a physician and a pathologist. Lynn this is Dr. Boardman, President Leonard's personal physician, and this is First Lady, Susan Leonard. I asked Lynn to join the autopsy team since she's an expert pathologist. Everyone, have a seat. Let's get started."

"One question we need answered, how did the President die, and why suddenly. To me, he looked healthy and in shape. Dr. Boardman, you and the President go back a while, do you have any ideas?"

"No sir I don't."

"Dr. I figured that. That's one of the reasons I asked Lynn here, because pathology is her specialty. She is also highly regarded in her field, and I value her opinion immensely. Having said that; Dr. Boardman I want you and Lynn to coordinate a comprehensive autopsy of the President. You may select three well qualified physicians to assist you. Members of the team must not discuss their work with anyone but me. If you need additional resources, you must send your requests directly to me and no one else. When you have finished your work, you are to deliver your report directly to me, no one else. I'll decide when the information should be released. Are we clear?"

"Yes sir."

"Then let's get started; your work must be completed by Friday evening. Lynn, stay a minute."

"Lynn have dinner with me, I need to talk to someone, just not about politics"
"John, I guess that will be alright."

"Good, I'll have Mrs. Witt show you where you'll be staying, and where we have dinner."

I now must speak with Amanda Jensen, the assistant press secretary, and Wayne Rogers, regarding funeral protocol for the late President. We need to let the First Lady know what items the government will handle. She will make the rest of the arrangements. If everything goes as planned, the President will lie in state in the Capitol rotunda from nine o'clock Saturday morning until seven o'clock Sunday night. The funeral will be at 1:30 on Monday. The next four days will be designated a national period of mourning.

My head is spinning uncontrollably; the last twelve hours have been nonstop. If I hear the words "Mr. President", I still look around for Andy Leonard; not fully realizing that I am the President. It seems I'm dealing with one crisis after another, which is true. When one gets resolved, another seems to pop up to take its place. The past eight years have been

*a world wind. First Mayor, then Governor, then
Vice President, and today President of the United
States, it is unreal. Maybe a good meal and some
Crown Royal will help relieve the tension. Now it's
on to Blair House to change clothes. For while it's
going to seem strange, working in the White House
as President, but living in the Vice Presidential
quarters.. It'll take the First Lady at least a couple
of weeks to locate another place to live.*

Lynn is waiting for me when I return. She has
changed clothes and let her hair down. Until now, I
never really looked at her; she is my sister-in-law,
which technically she is not.

*She looks beautiful. Her dress matches her blue
eyes, her hair a flowing light brown.*

"Lynn thanks for coming on such short notice,
given the circumstances. You realize you just have
one day to examine the President's body, on
Saturday he will be taken to the Capitol."

"Enough of that now, would you care to join me for a drink, I could use one?"

"Okay. John, or should I call you Mr. President?"

"John is fine. John, how are you holding up, the stress must be tremendous?"

"I'll be okay it's just going to take time to adjust to a different set of demands"

"John would you like me to rub your shoulders; you seem tense?"

"Are you sure, I don't want to put you out?

"It is okay, I'm a doctor; remember."

The past year has been busy I really haven't had time to date. Maybe Lynn and I are more alike than I thought. Maybe in the coming days, I'll know why.

"Lynn let's eat, the chef is fixing pan-fried walleye, steamed vegetables and fresh dinner rolls."

"John that sounds great."

Day Two

Friday March 1, 3am

Only 3:00, it's not time to get up; five hours is hardly enough sleep but I guess that's all I'm going get. I still can't believe I am President; a real dream. The past twenty-four hours were unbelievable. Soon the Secret Service will be picking me up for a quick ride to the White House. Harry Truman and I share this 'journey', a two-minute ride instead of a six-minute walk. It will be a while before I move in, so I best get use to it. Now for a warm shower to wake me up; this time I won't forget the soap.

Many people may think I'm not smart enough, the Cabinet, the Congress, and the White House staff among them. Although when I came here as Vice President I was determined to learn and read everything I could get my hands on. My studies included State and Defense Department briefs, the Congressional Record, internal memos, and a host of letters. If there were decisions to be made I was prepared to make them. Although under our system of government, the Vice President makes almost none. Still President Leonard tutored me as if I would one day.

President Leonard often told me his job was a lonely one; now I know what he was talking about. Two more issues now need my attention. First, the Chairman of the Joints Chief of Staff is waiting to brief me on overnight developments in the Middle East; I'm prepared for the worst but I can handle it; having studied the situation for some time. Also my sister-in-law, Lynn, the doctor is having problems. It seems her colleagues are giving her a hard time on how to do the procedure. First the autopsy issue.

"Dr. Boardman, come into my office, I want to talk to you. Boardman, your job along with your colleagues, is to perform a comprehensive autopsy on the President, and when concerns arise, I want all of you to be open to differing points of view and take advice when offered. Lynn has particular expertise in forensic science, so I suggest you and the others listen to what she has to say, she knows what she is talking about. Okay doctor."

"I understand Mr. President."

Lynn is present and heard what I said. She appears shocked by my words.

"John is that how presidents handle things?"

"Lynn, there is only boss; and that's me, despite what some might think."

"Admiral Timm, are you here to talk about the Middle East or something else?"

"Sir, the answer is yes on both counts."

I knew the answer by looking at his face, but with military people you never know for sure.

"Mr. President, Major General David Loveday, head of the Army's Special Forces, is joining us and will present his plan for the invasion of Syria."

President Leonard had mentioned the plan to me several weeks before he died. The plan or mission, as I understand it, involves four special operation teams from the Army and Navy, some four hundred soldiers all totaled. The teams will invade Syria from strategic locations. The Air Force, for its part, would provide air support. The primary objective is to overthrow the Adii government. Despite the complexity of the mission, casualties are believed to be relatively small, numbering no more than one hundred and fifty Syrian soldiers and less than a hundred civilians. If I choose to approve the plan, the operation would begin five days from now.

"General Loveday, when did President Leonard authorize planning for this mission?"

"Sir, the President, Admiral Timm, National Security Advisor Herb Williams and I discussed the operation on three occasions."

"General, when did he approve it?"

"Mr. President, he gave me verbal approval last week; I don't recall the exact day."

"General, President Leonard and I discussed your idea on two occasions, the last time on Monday. I'll tell you, each of us had reservations. Since I came to Washington, I've spent a considerable amount of time studying the Middle East and read most if not all the analytical reports on the region. Without a doubt, Syria is in trouble, but military action is not the answer. As surgical as the operation appears, we have to consider the long-range effects this action will have, and they will be significant. I have no doubt the mission—the invasion--will be a success in the short term; it's the occupation and the effects of it that bother me the most. Having said that, I am not prepared to pay that price, at least not yet. For the next few days, let's focus on mourning the loss of President Leonard. I'm confident the situation will not change during that time. We'll revisit the matter ten days from today, in the interim

General work on a logistical update and have it ready for my review by next Friday."

"Very well Mr. President."

"Good day men."

"Admiral Timm, do you have a couple of minutes."

"Of course, I do Mr. President."

"Sir, President Leonard mentioned you plan to retire at the end of March."

"Yes, sir I am."

"Do you have plans after that?"

"Sir, no I don't, at least nothing is definite."

"Did you know President Leonard was planning to offer you a job?"

"No Mr. President I did not."

"Admiral, I'd like you to come work for me as my senior advisor on counter terrorism. I've looked over your record, and I'm confident you're the right man for the job."

"Mr. President, I don't know what to say."

"Well, talk it over with Mrs. Timm and let's talk again next week.

"Okay Admiral."

"Okay sir."

Now I can enjoy the rest of the day, in relative peace, although calm often precedes a storm. I can feel it in my bones. Before retiring I'm going to play my favorite pieces on the piano, exercise, and read the daily reports. Tomorrow will be as chaotic as today was peaceful. I wonder if the Secret Service will let me walk to Blair House; it's idiotic to drive there, the walk takes about six minutes. Maybe I'll try out the piano in the East Room; it's a baby grand.

This piano is marvelous, what tone; the range is unbelievable. Then I hear the door open. It's Sgt. Hills, a marine guard assigned to the White House.

"Who the hell is playing the piano, no one is suppose to be in here."

The Sgt. can't see me from where he is standing.

"Sgt, it okay, it's only me, President Keller."

"Sir, I'm sorry, I didn't know you were in here. By the way you play beautifully."

"Thank you, but I'm done now. Please let the Secret Service know I wish to go to Blair House."

"Yes, sir right away"

Now I suppose the rumor mill will be critiquing my playing ability, I guess it comes with the territory.

Day Three
Saturday March 2 10:30 am

"Mrs. Witt, can you come in here, I want to review my appointment schedule."

"Yes, but shouldn't we meet in the Oval Office, you're the President now."

"Thanks for reminding me madam; but since we're both here, the Cabinet Room will suffice. Who's on the schedule for this afternoon?"

"Mr. President, you have a one o'clock appointment with the Attorney General; a two o'clock with the Secretary of State; a three o'clock with the Vice Presidential staff, and at four thirty you have a meeting with your sister-in-law."

"Good, please ask the White House Chef to have dinner ready at six o'clock, Lynn is joining me. One more thing, get my son and daughter on the phone; I need to talk to them."

"Mr. President."

"What is it Mrs. Witt?"

"Sir, I almost forgot, Senator Pearson is outside and wants to talk to you; she says its important but didn't say why."

"Okay, tell her I can give her a few minutes, but once you have my kids on the phone, I'll end it."

That's just great, time with Senator "hot pants.

People call her that because she can't seem to keep her pants up. Rumor has it she's slept with nearly half of the male Senators and a couple dozen Congressmen. I first met her last September, during a formal dinner at the White House; I recall she was extremely forward and brash. After a few minutes of listening to her, I simply walked away. We have not spoken since.

"Senator Pearson, nice to see you, what can I do?"
"For starters drop the Senator, call me Jacki."
"Great, you can call me Mr. President. Now what did you need that's so important?"

"I just wanted to say, I'm here to offer my help and support if you need it."

"Thank you, now if you'll excuse me, Mrs. Witt is signaling my children are now on the phone."

As I reach for the phone, Miss **hot pants** turns around, shrugging her shoulders, swinging her hips and strutting away; in a huff. It's been a long time since I had sex, and if I asked her, I'm sure she would oblige, but she's not my type. The last thing I need is an affair.

"Dad, are you there?"

"Kids, did you all have a nice vacation?"

"Dad we did."

"Elizabeth it's nice to hear your voice. I apologize for not calling you sooner, but I wasn't sure how to reach you; things have been very hectic here."

"Dad, how are you holding up?"

"Great, David."

"Dad we were worried about you."

"Elizabeth I'm okay. I'm more worried about you and your brother and your children. Very soon reporters and photographers will be snooping around your place, asking questions, looking for a story. Sadly, those people don't care if they disrupt your life. You'll also see more Secret Service agents around, now that I am President."
"Oh before I forget, my secretary has plane tickets for you, David, and the kids. I believe your flight leaves tomorrow morning, but she'll call you with the details. If you can, I'd like you to stay until Tuesday, if that's alright."

"That's okay Dad."

"Dad, I wish Mom was here."

"Honey so do I, but I suspect she's watching us all the same."

"Dad is Lynn at the White House with you?"

"Yes, David she is; I'll fill you in on the details when you get here. Kids, I have to hang up now, people are waiting to see me."

"Dad your grandchildren would like to say hi before you hang up."

"Grandpa, are you really the President."

"Yes, Susie I am."

"Grandpa, can I sit in your chair?"

"Jack sure you can."

"Sorry kids I have to go see you all tomorrow; the Attorney General is waiting to see me."

"Mr. Attorney General, thanks for meeting me on such short notice, it has been hectic around here to say the least."

"Sir, I bet it has."

"Russ what kind of rumblings are you hearing regarding the President death?"

"Mr. President, most people are asking how it happened and why."

"Any mention of foul play or questions regarding the autopsy?" "No."

"Good. If anything, suspicious is uncovered, and I hope it's not, things may get tense. In any case, I plan to keep a firm grip regardless of the outcome."

"Sir, I know you will, you have my full support." "Thanks Russ. When I receive the preliminary results, I'll let you know. Are you available this evening if I need you?"

"Yes sir, just let me know."

"Mr. President."

"Yes, what is Mrs. Witt?"

"The Secretary of State is waiting to see you."

"Madam Secretary; thanks for coming."

"Mr. President what can I do for you?"

"First, I need a brief assessment on how our allies and our enemies have reacted to the President's death and their impression of me but wait to prepare it until after the funeral."

"Mr. President, we have received condolences from all over the world; the response has been overwhelming. Sir, with your permission, I'd like to arrange a meeting with the foreign dignitaries, probably for tomorrow afternoon."

"That would be fine."

Madam Secretary, how about the intelligence sector, do they have concerns?"

"Sir, none right now but they're constantly on the alert for any threats that might develop."

"Vicky, the next few days will be chaotic; if you need anything, anything at all, just ask."

"Sir, I will, and you the same".

"Sir, the Vice- Presidential staff are here, should I send them in?"

"Thank you, Mrs. Witt; yes, but give me a few minutes; I need a moment to collect my thoughts.

"Sir, will you need me for anything else?"

"No, I don't think so."
When I came to Washington, I inherited all but one person. Ben Johnson, the only exception, he started working for me when I first elected Governor. I hate to lose him, he is a good man, but what assignment is good for him, he has only been in Washington a few months. President Leonard's staff, all veterans.

"People thanks for coming on such short notice. I'm going to be frank with you, so I'll get right to the point. Since assuming this job I've had no time to think about assignments. Things have been too hectic. I wish I could promise all of you a job, but right now, I can't. For the next several weeks I'm going to have you work with the Presidential staff. It could be several months before a new Vice President is in office. That person will make the final decision on staff makeup. Does anyone have any questions?"

"Sir I think I speak for everyone here, you have our complete support, if you need anything, anything at all, and we're here to assist you."

"Thank you Ben I appreciate that, now if you'll excuse me, I've other matters to attend to."
"Mrs. Witt let me know when my sister-in-law arrives; in the meantime, I'm going to study some reports and make a few notes."

"Mr. President the First Lady is here and wants to talk to you, she said she needs only a minute."

"Okay, send her in."
"John, how are you doing?"

"I should be asking you that question; I'm okay."

"Mr. President have you gotten any reports on Andy's autopsy?"

"No, I haven't, maybe by this evening. Now, is there anything else?"

"John I'd like you to sing at the President's funeral."

"Sue, are you sure, I haven't sung before a live audience in years; I need time to practice."

"I understand. You know, Andy told me he heard you sing on several occasions and enjoyed listening to you."

"Sue before I accept, I have to test my voice, if it's not up to it I must decline."

"John how much time do you need?"

"Give me until tomorrow afternoon, by then I should know. In the meantime, don't discuss this with anyone, only a few people know I sing; the gossips don't need a story, a story that might otherwise distract from the President's funeral."

"John I'll make sure your name is listed just for the eulogy. I'll also ask the orchestra not to discuss who might be singing."

"Sue I hope it works out, and unless you have something else, I have to let you go."

Keller, where is your head, sing before millions of people, if you mess up, your presidency is in trouble even before it begins. Still if I pull it off, people might think of me differently and stop referring to me as that fellow from the Midwest.

"Lynn, come in, what do you know?"

"My preliminary analysis of the President's blood suggests he died from a rare form of bacteria."
"Can you identify it? What's it is, is it bad stuff?"

"Yes Mr. President. The Center for Disease Control identified it last year; it's called BA3-19. A few months after that, they discovered it could mutate under the right conditions. Mutated bacteria can be very deadly."

"For the moment, let's not worry about labels, what I want to know, did it kill the President, and if so, how did it enter his body?"

"Mr. President, I can't say this particular strain caused his death by itself, but if the right condition were present in his blood, it certainly could have been a contributor."

"Are there any more tests or procedures you need to do before the wake? "

"No."

"Is there any chance of an epidemic?"

"My intuition suggests no, but with bacteria you never know for sure."

"Lynn let me be clear, you cannot discuss this with anyone until we know more."

"Lynn, now that the autopsy is over, what are your plans; go home, stay for the funeral? Elizabeth, David, and the grandkids are coming tomorrow, I'm sure they would love to see you."

"John, how long do they plan to stay?"

"I asked them to stay until Tuesday."

"Mr. President, I'll stay until they get here."

"Lynn, when we're alone, call me John. Now if you'll excuse me, I must make a few phone calls, then head for Blair House for a little study time. I'll back around seven. Join me for dinner?"

"Yes, I'd love to, but why can't you study here?"

"Lynn, the First Lady asked me to sing at the President's funeral, so I need to practice, privately."

"John, I didn't know you could sing."

"Most people don't. When I was an undergraduate, I studied opera for several years, but chose not to pursue it, professionally; it's been three years since I last sang before a live audience, and it was a small one at that. I must let the First Lady know by tomorrow afternoon if I'm up to it. I certainly don't want to mess up in front of millions of people."
"I completely understand, but if you pull it off, think of the adulation."

"I know that's what worries me."

"What are you going to sing?"
"Ava Maria."

Now off to Blair House. As I open the door house the voice of doubt enters my mind.

Keller, do I really want to do this, sing before millions of people? Think of the consequences, I'd be the laughing stock of the world, not to mention embarrassing my family and the President's. Stop it, it's time to stop whining and get to work. Now where did I leave my sheet music and background CD? Here goes nothing.

Not bad, let me do it again, and again, and again. Now that's over with, I think it's time to record it and play it back.

Okay I think, but if practice several more hours it could do it even better, but I don't have the luxury. Supper time is near at hand, time to get back to the White House and clean up. I'm looking forward to getting Lynn's reaction, at least I think so.

"Lynn now that you've had a good meal and had time to relax, I want you to listen to something. Well what do you think?"

"John, beautiful, you have a fantastic voice."
"You aren't just saying that to be nice; it's my head on the line?"

"No, I am not. John, sit down, I need to tell you something. Just before my sister died she asked me a very important question. She said, Lynn if John ever gets in a tight spot and needs help can you be there for him? Can you do that for me? Regrettably, I didn't give her an answer, but I'm giving you mine now, my answer is yes."

"Lynn I don't know what to say."

"Don't say anything just give me a hug and hold me tight. Lynn, don't take this wrong, but I have to go, I need to study some reports and prepare for a meeting with the heads of state."

"Okay John."

The situation in the Middle East does not look good. It seems not a week goes by before one group tries to destroy another. Historically, no one has gotten along for any length of time. Fighting appears to be a "way of life". I think it comes down to control, who has it and who wants to have it. Legitimacy appears to emanate within religious demagoguery. This is too much to absorb now, I still have a fifty-page State Department brief in front of me. Maybe I can find something positive, at least I hope so.

Day Four

Sunday March 3 5:25 am

"Mr. President, are you awake?"

"Yes, George what is it?"

"Admiral Timm is on the phone, and he says he needs to talk to you right away."

"Tell him to hold on, I need a few minutes to clear my head."

I must look like hell, and my back hurts to.

"George, get me a washcloth and a glass of water; you're my steward now, aren't you?"

"Mr. President, I am."

"Admiral, what can I do for you?"

"Sir, is Mrs. Witt coming into work this morning?"

"I think so; she usually comes in around seven.

Why do you ask?"

"Sir, the plane her son was flying, crashed during flight operations, off the carrier Eisenhower."
"What happened?"

"The arresting wire broke as he was landing, his plane slid into the water as a result."

"Were they able to recover him?"

"Yes, but he died shortly after; the ejection seat had propelled him straight into the water; the force broke his neck. Sir, I thought you should be one to break the news to her."

"I will, but I want you and the White House chaplain to be there when I tell her. Meet me in my office at 6:45."

How do you tell a mother she just lost a son? The thought of it, bothers to no end.

"Admiral, chaplain do come in. Mrs. Witt, please come in. Everyone, have a seat."

"What is it Mr. President?
Last night, there was an accident onboard the Eisenhower and your son's plane crashed."

"Sir, is he alright? No Mrs. Witt; the crash broke his neck and he died shortly thereafter."

"What happened?"

"The arresting wire broke as he was landing, as a result his plane slid off the flight deck; by the time his ejection seat fired, his plane had already turned over on its side, the force drove him into the sea."

"Did they recover his body?"

"Yes. I'm so sorry; chaplain could you please take Mrs. Witt to the chapel."

"Mr. President, I should stay here, who's going to help you?"

"Don't worry about me; you need to be with your family; I've asked the Admiral to dispatch a plane to pick up your daughter, your son-in-law, and your grand children so they can be with you during this difficult time."

"George will you contact the head of the Secret Service; tell him I plan to attend church this morning. It will be the 10:30 service; my family will be joining me. Also, call my sister-in-law and tell her to come over as soon as she can."

"Yes, right away sir."

"Thanks George. Admiral, can you arrange a meeting with the Joint Chiefs, the Defense Secretary and my foreign affairs advisors, for 3:00 this afternoon."

"Sir, I'll take care of it."

"Thanks Admiral, now if you'll excuse me, I need to make a few phone calls."

"Sue, John Keller, could you come to my office at nine, I need to update you on a few items"

"Mr. President, I'll be there."

"Okay, see you then."

"Mr. Attorney General could you meet me in my office at 9:15, Doctor Boardman will join us around 9:20. Can you make it?" "Yes."

As I hang up the phone, Lynn walks in.
"Good morning Lynn, please come in, have a seat. Today is not off to a good start. Just before six I found out Mrs. Witt's son was killed in plane crash, and I had to break the news to her."

"John, no, how is she taking it?"

"I'm not sure she's hard to read; now the reason I called you here. The First Lady is joining us at 9:15, the Attorney General and Doctor Boardman a few minutes later; together we're going to talk about the autopsy. However, before they arrive, I want to hear about your findings; specifically, have you determined the precise cause of death. Oh, before I forget, Elizabeth, David and the kids will be here at ten; then head for church, I'd like you to join us.

Okay."

"Well John, we know the President was exposed to a rare form of bacteria, and I believe that bacteria mutated, for reasons I don't fully understand. Maybe the President had a specific health condition that caused a mutation. I haven't read his health history, so I can't be sure with complete certainty."

"Lynn, what are the sources of the bacteria, and how could it have gotten into his blood?"

"Regarding possible sources, I don't know of any off hand; second he most likely inhaled it. There were no puncture wounds on his body. Maybe

Doctor Boardman or Mrs. Leonard could shed some light on the subject."

"Speaking of the First Lady, here she is now."

"Sue, how are you doing?"

"Okay I guess, given all that has happened."
"Sue, this is my sister-in-law Lynn; she's a pathologist from Minnesota, and she was part of the team that examined the President. Lynn, tell the First Lady what we know up to this point."

"Mrs. Leonard, let me begin by saying, we don't know for sure what caused your husband's death. We do know he was exposed to a rare form of bacteria, which for some reason mutated in his body and may have contributed to his death, but only if the right underlying health conditions were present. Was your husband in good health, and do you know if he took medication for a particular condition(s)?"

"As far as I know, the President was in good health, although he was taking several blood pressure medications, and low dosage aspirin."

"Thank you Mrs. Leonard; let's wait and see if Doctor Boardman has anything to add.

"Oh, Sue before I forget, I'm up for singing at Andy's funeral. Would you mind if I do it the after my eulogy?"

"That's fine."

"Also tell the orchestra conductor I need some practice time that morning. He can schedule them when it's convenient for him."

"John, I really appreciate your help; and about your requests, consider them handled."

"Sue, Lynn, please excuse me, I want to see if Boardman and the Attorney General are here."

"Mr. Attorney General, this is my sister-in-law Lynn, she assisted the medical team with the autopsy. Lynn, please update Doctor Boardman."

"Doctor Boardman, my analysis of the President's blood indicates the presence of a rare form of bacteria, identified as BA3-19. We don't know very much about this particular bacteria, it was only recently discovered; and so far we haven't observed a case where the bacteria mutated; but in the President's case, it did. We believe the bacteria are generally harmless, even if it mutates although we can't be one hundred percent certain. However, if mutation occurs, its effects can be different. Furthermore we suspect that if someone has the right medical condition(s), combined with the mutation, an adverse reaction might result. Doctor was the President in good health; and was he taking medication?"

"Lynn, the President was taking medication for high blood pressure, and sleep apnea".

"Sir, can you tell me specifically what those drugs were and the dosage?"

"Right now, I can't tell you what they are off the top of my head."

"Sir, when did he have his last physical?"
"Nine months ago, I believe."

"Could you provide me a copy of that report; it could help me form some conclusions."

"I can give you all the information you need, just come by my office when we're finished here."

"Thanks, I will doctor."

"Mr. President, any questions?"

"No Lynn I don't. Okay everyone, I need to speak to the Attorney General, alone. Doctor Boardman, Lynn, please wait for him outside; he'll join you in a few minutes."

"Mr. Attorney General, what do you think?"

"Mr. President, it seems a little strange."

"I concur.   I'd like you to review the President's appointment schedule and meeting log for the past ten days and interview all the Secret Service agents on duty during that period. Maybe he went somewhere unusual, if so, we need to know about it. One thing more, I want you to accompany my sister-in-law to Boardman's office, and have the Secret Service assign her an agent. Maybe I'm being too cautious, but I'm not taking any chances."

"Good idea sir."

"Lynn, the Attorney General will walk with you, and don't forget about church."

Now I need a few minutes alone.

"Mrs. Witt what are you doing here?"

"Mr. President, Bill O'Brien is on the phone, he says it's important."

"Okay, but why are you here, you should be with your family."

"Sir, I can't do anything for Richard, and my family says I need to keep busy."

"Now I wonder what Bill wants; he isn't the kind of person to call and shoot the breeze."

Bill is head of the Department of Earth Science and Geology at the University of Minnesota. We met at an educational symposium, when I was Governor. Eventually we became good friends, but since I came to Washington, we haven't spoken.

"Bill, how are you, it's been a while?"

"John, I mean Mr. President, just fine. I know you're extremely busy so I'll get right to the point. For the last ninety-six hours, we've been tracking major seismic activity in Eastern Europe and the central United States. At first, we thought the disturbances would be short lived. Instead, they have been increasing at an alarming rate."

"Bill, what does your gut tell you?"

"John, there will be a catastrophic earthquake in eastern Europe, starting at the southwest tip of Russia, running through the Black Sea, and Arabic peninsula, possibly reaching India and Pakistan. Here in the Central US, we believe a smaller quake will strike Missouri, Arkansas, Tennessee, and Kentucky, if you call that smaller."

"Bill, how certain?"

"Seventy-five percent is my guess. I've already talked to my colleagues at St. Louis University and Moscow University, and they concur with my findings. How much time do we have to prepare? My guess and it is only a guess, three or four days, in Europe, maybe less."

"Bill, I'm going to arrange a joint conference this afternoon to discuss the situation, hopefully we can develop a specific course of action, and can you be available?"

"Yes sir, anything you need."

"Thanks Bill, I have to go, I'm late for church."

"Mr. President, your family is here."

"Tell them I'll be right out, first I have to make a quick phone call."

"Madam Secretary, John Keller."

"Yes sir, what can I do for you?"

"I need you to contact Wayne Roberts, the Speaker of the House, the Senate Majority Leader, the Defense Secretary, Admiral Timm, the Governors of Missouri, Arkansas, Tennessee, and Kentucky, the Secretary of Homeland Security, the Treasury Secretary, and the Press Secretary, and set up an emergency meeting in the Cabinet Room for 2:30 this afternoon. The governors will be joining us via satellite, as will the scientists. I also want you to call Dr. Bill O'Brien at the University of Minnesota; Mrs. Witt has his number, tell him to have his colleagues join us at that time. Vickie, this matter has the highest priority; I need your full cooperation. I don't have time to explain, be in my office at 1:30 and I'll try to elaborate."

"Elizabeth, David, kids, good to see you; did you have a good trip?" "Dad, grandpa; how are you?" "I'm fine given the circumstances; let's head for church." "Dad, what is it?" "I'll tell you later."

As the minister delivers his sermon, I can't help but think about the people that will be affected by those earthquakes; I know how much my family means to me; a fact at times I overlooked as Governor, and as Vice President. I'm not going to let that happen again. I must remain strong, I am the President. I know nothing can prevent horrific acts of nature from taking place.

"Dad, the service is over." I hadn't noticed; my mind is elsewhere.

"Elizabeth, David walk with me, let Agent Davis take the children."

"Dad what is it?"

"Before I say anything, I want both of you to agree not to say anything, to anyone, about I'm going to tell you, I mean nobody? Elizabeth."
"I won't." "David."I won't."

"Do you remember Dr. Bill O'Brien from the University of Minnesota?"

"Yes. He's a professor of geology I think."

"That's right. Well Bill called me this morning with some disturbing news. For the past few days, Bill and his colleagues at the California Institute of Seismology have been tracking major disturbances in the Earth, here in the Unites States and in Middle East. They believe, if these disturbances continue, that two major earthquakes will evolve. The one in the Middle East could cause mass destruction in the Black Sea and Persian Gulf regions. In the United

States, the states of Missouri, Arkansas, Kentucky and Tennessee will be affected. A major quake in the Middle East could send oil prices thru the roof and possibly put the financial markets in a downward spiral. In our country, besides the financial affects from the Middle East quake, many Americans could be killed, many more injured; some severely. The potential destruction in the urban areas, horrific."

"Dad, when will it happen?"

"We don't know for sure, but it could be within the next seventy-two to ninety-six hours."

"Dad, what are you going to do, what's your plan?"

"This afternoon we're having a meeting with elected officials, staff, and the scientific community to discuss what we can do to minimize the impact."

"What can we do? "

"You kids can give me emotional support; I will need plenty of it."

"Dad, count on it."

"By the way, I didn't see your Aunt in church, I asked her to join us. Here is her cell number. Could you call her? Tell her I'll call her later, and don't mention what I told you. We don't need rumors flying around."

"Dad, it's okay, we're on top of it."

"Is it already twelve thirty, I have to go. I'll have Mrs. Witt call you with dinner arrangements."

"Mrs. Witt, hold all calls, I need time to prepare for this afternoon's meeting."

If I don't have an outline, we'll never get anything done. I think we should consider a multi tier scenario: starting with a moderate event, inclusive of two subsets, one for Europe and one for the US. Bill and his colleagues can provide an overview.

Following that, we need to discuss how we can minimize causalities and injuries. That sounds good, now onto the meeting.

"Ladies and men, thank you for joining me. I don't have to tell you, these are troubling times. This morning I received word we might be facing another crisis. It will affect many people and could change our way of life. At this point, I'm not certain if or when it might happen, nor what the outcomes will be, if it does. One thing I do know, we have to remain strong, all of us. We don't have time for political bickering; we must work together. Dr. Bill O'Brien, Professor of Earth Science and Geology at the University of Minnesota, will now present an overview of the situation as it now stands; Dr. O'Brien."

"Mr. President."

"For the past week, my colleagues at the University of Minnesota and the California Institute of Seismology have observed an unusually large build up of seismic energy in the south-central part of the United States and in the Middle East, principally in the Black Sea region. Initially we thought this activity, although strong, would eventually diminish, but that hasn't happened. In fact, the energy level has risen, at the alarming rate of five percent per hour, for three consecutive days. If that trend continues, our models indicate there'll be a major earthquake in the areas shown on the map. The energy will top 9.4 on the Richter scale. In the U.S., a quake of 9.0 in the southern Mississippi River Valley basin could have a path of destruction 200 - 300 miles long and 50 - 100 miles wide. Understand, these are estimates, and are based on facts we have now; it's what we don't know that concerns me more. I can't even say for sure the seismic activity will continue to grow at its present rate, we just don't know. In the Middle East, uncertainty is about the same. We do know that if there is an earthquake in that region, greater than 9.1, underground oil supplies will definitely be impacted, as will key waterways."

"Dr. O'Brien, Admiral Timm, Chairman of the Joint Chief Staff, can you tell us what cities will be affected in the US?"

"Admiral, in Missouri everything south and east of St Louis and possibly St. Louis, may sustain heavy damage. In Arkansas, most everything north and east of Little Rock, would suffer heavy damage as well, but the city itself less so. In Kentucky, everything south and west of Bowling-Green, is also in the quake area however damage could be less severe. Tennessee would not be so lucky. Everything west of Jackson, especially Memphis, could be seriously affected."

"Dr. O'Brien, what about deaths and injuries?"
"Admiral I haven't reviewed the projections, but I'm guessing it would be a lot. Understand, we' haven't seen activity this big in my lifetime, as such we are not entirely certain how precise our models are. We don't need to panic, however, the data is real; that's why I contacted the President, and then he called you here this afternoon. Dr. Allen, my

colleague in California, has prepared some multi tiered models, covering moderate to severe destruction for both areas. The first three cover the Mississippi River Valley basin, the last three the Middle East. If these quakes do occur, they will happen sometime within the next three, possibly five days, but that's just an estimate. Mr. President."

"Thank you, Dr. O'Brien."

I can't believe what I just heard. As I look around the room everyone appears to be in shock. How do we get our hands around this? When do we warn people, what do we tell them?

The first thing we should consider is evacuation. Is evacuation possible, and if so where do we direct the people, how will they be cared for, and where will they go when it's all over? Logistically, I don't think we have time to prepare. I'm sure we could relocate some, but who do we leave behind, and if we get them out, can we have a settlement site ready in time, is that even possible?

"Mr. President." "Secretary Johnson."

"Sir, given the time constraints I don't think we can do a meaningful evacuation. Mr. President, I think we should prepare for the after effects, assuming the quake strikes."

"Governors, how should we approach this?"
"John, Governor Murray, evacuation is out of question; we simply don't have the resources to do it in such a short amount of time. First, I suggest we tell people how to protect one another, if there is an earthquake. Second, if it does occur, response must be to the hardest hit areas. Our response should entail opening roadways, supplying water, food, medical supplies and rescue personnel. Farm fields would be a perfect site for relocation camps for those displaced. Every camp must have a triage center to treat the injured; persons needing additional care could be airlifted to regional medical centers. State National Guard commanders should be able to coordinate activities with the help of the

Secretary of Homeland Security and the Secretary of the Army."

"Governor Murray, what else should the Federal Government do?"

"Sir, active duty military personnel could assist the National Guard in rescue efforts; Navy Seabees could handle infrastructure problems; and your administration could help recruit medical personnel from other parts of the country. The Air Force could provide the necessary aircraft, and lastly and most importantly, food suppliers and drug companies should be asked to donate food and medical supplies. I know it sounds like we're preparing for war, in a way we are."

"Len, I agree with you. Governor Petersen."

"I agree with Len."

"Governor Edwards, Governor Jensen what do you guys think? Governor Edwards."

"Sir when do we get started?"

"Just as soon as this meeting is over, we have about forty-eight hours to prepare. I know, that's not much time, but we simply have none to spare."

"Mr. President. Governor Jensen."

"Who is going to pay for all of this?"

"We all are; we're in this together, and if I hear of anyone taking advantage of the situation, I will hold them personally accountable. Now we'll reconvene at 5 o'clock tomorrow to evaluate how we're doing in, as outlined. Dr. O'Brien will send you updates when they become available. Thank you all."

"Mr. Roberts, Secretary Johnson, Secretary Coles, Admiral Timm, Mr. Attorney General, please stay, we need to talk over a few things regarding the Middle East. Dr. O'Brien will join us."

"Dr. O'Brien."

"Mr. President I'll be brief and to the point. The seismic activity we're seeing in the Middle East is very dangerous. I'd like to show you three possible outcomes. All three will likely follow the same path; that is from southwest Russia near the northeast corner of the Black Sea, and south southeasterly along the border between Iran and Iraq, through the Persian Gulf, through the Gulf of Oman, east to an area near Karachi India. A moderate quake, say 6 to 7 on the Richter scale may impact underground oil supplies, produce some flooding and affect certain shipping lanes. A major quake, say 9.1 or higher, could double the impact. If that happens, the economic fallout for the region and perhaps the world could be astronomical."

"Dr., Wayne Roberts, how likely will a quake of any magnitude occur and when?"

"Sir, probably a ninety percent chance; and it could happen within the next 72-96 hours. This of course depends on whether the activity continues to grow at its present pace. The quake, if it happens, will start three to four miles below the earth's surface. We know very little about quakes at that depth; the last one, as far as we know, occurred about 150,000 years ago. Given the potential severity, I wanted to alert you. Mr. President."

"Thank you, Dr. O'Brien." "People, if a quake occurs here and in the Middle East, I surmise the world's energy and financial markets will be impacted. No one can prevent the quakes from happening; what we can do is prepare in advance to lessen the effects. Secretary Coles what can/should we do to protect capital and oil reserves?"

"Mr. President, first, I would shift most of our overseas assets, especially currency, to more stable environments. Second, I would suspend Wall Street trading for at least five business days. Third, I would halt oil and natural gas exports, exports not otherwise loaded and ready for shipment. Finally, I would appeal to the American people and the business community to remain calm and be patient as we work through this difficult situation."

"Thank you, Mr. Secretary."

"Does anyone else have a comment or suggestions? Secretary Johnson, what should Homeland Security be doing?"

"Sir, we must maintain order. My agency will coordinate our emergency response with all local and state law enforcement agencies, as well as the National Guard."

"Amanda Jensen, how should we handle the media? Rumors may be the order of the day."

"Sir, once the quake hits, I suggest you call the heads of the major radio, television, and newspaper organizations, and express the paramount need to act responsibly."

"Amanda, that's asking a lot."

"Sir, I know, but I think it's important we try nonetheless."

"Admiral Timm, I want you to work directly with Wayne Rogers and the Attorney General to assure all provisions are carried out. I'll see everyone back here tomorrow afternoon. Mr. Attorney General, was someone permanently assigned to protect my sister-in-law?"

"Yes sir, he's one of our best. In fact, he's outside with her now."

"Thank you."

"Mrs. Witt, please contact my children and ask them to come to the White House for dinner. Lynn, come in, have you been waiting long?"

"Not long, only about five minutes."

"Did you learn anything new after studying the President's medical history?"

"Nothing conclusive; it might help if I knew where he was the last couple of days prior to his death, and who he was with yesterday."

"The Attorney General is working on it, but we may not know anything for several more days. How long can you stay?"

"I have to leave Tuesday morning. I'll let you know if I find out anything new."

"John you look tried." "It's been a rough day."

As she walks towards me, I notice she is staring right at me; she has never done that before. It looks quite passionate, and empathic. Watching her movements, it's obvious I'm staring back; it's been a long time.

"John, can I rub your back, it could help you relax?"

Just as she was about to begin, the kids walk in.

"We're here, hi Dad, hi Grandpa, hi Lynn."
"Hi kids." "John I'm going to clean up; later."

"Dad, what's up?" "What do you mean?"
"I saw how Lynn was looking at you, and the look you gave her."

"We both had a long day; it was nothing." "Sure."
"If it bothers you honey, why don't you ask her?" "I
just might do that."

"You know Dad, Mom has been gone for a long
time; it's time to get on with your life you're still
quite young."

"Honey, I'm going shower and change clothes;
dinner is at 6:30"

*In the shower, I couldn't help but think about what
Elizabeth said. Was grief preventing me from
having a relationship, had I buried myself in work?
The answer is, probably yes, on both counts, but
Presidents aren't supposed to have romantic
encounters are they, and definitely not during a
crisis. Now enough of that, I must prepare for the
funeral; I have a speech to deliver and an aria to
sing, that's where my head should be; she is
beautiful though, and legally no longer a relative.*

Day Five

Monday March 4 5:45 am

Its morning, was that a good night's sleep or what. What time is rehearsal; oh yes 8:30. Now on to breakfast; then practice before heading to church. Is that the phone?

"Secretary Conrad—Commerce Secretary Vickie Conrad--how are you."

"Not good Mr. President, things are heating up."

"What's happening?"

"About an hour ago, the Russian new agency released a statement regarding a possible earthquake near the Black Sea. They said a massive quake, of epic proportions, may devastate the region sometime within the next two or three days; and as a result of their statement, we're starting to see a little turmoil brewing, mostly in the oil producing countries."

"Did they mention anything about our quake?

No sir they didn't.

Vickie, it appears I'll have to deal with that situation right away; I'm going to move up the afternoon meeting to 1:30, keep me posted. Mrs. Witt, get Wayne Rogers on the phone."

"Wayne, this is the President, get a hold of everyone who was at yesterday's meeting and tell them to be in the Situation Room at 1:30; all hell is breaking loose in the Middle East; also tell the Press Secretary to call me right away. Here we go."

"Mr. President, Press Secretary Edwards is on the phone. Do you wish to speak to him?"

"Martin, when can you get here?"

"Sir I can be there in ten minutes."

"Martin, have a seat. Chaos has begun in the Middle East, and the quake hasn't even hit. I want you to draft a speech on the subject; I plan on delivering it tonight. For some reason, President

Leonard's speechwriter is out of town, and you're the only one I can ask on such short notice. Here's an outline to help you."

"Sir, are you sure you want me to write it, I've written speeches before, none like this."

"Martin you'll do just fine, following this afternoon's emergency meeting, we can go over it together and fine tune it."

"Okay sir."

"Martin I also want you to call all the major radio and television networks and request thirty minutes of airtime; schedule it for 8:00 (PM) EST. Oh, one more thing, the meeting scheduled for late this afternoon was moved up to 1:30; see you then."

Darn, look at the time; less than an hour to rehearse the eulogy and practice the aria; but first I need to sit down; everything is happening too fast. For starters, I have to bid my good friend, the

*President, an emotional goodbye. If that's not
traumatic enough, right after that I have to sing Ava
Maria before a worldwide audience; I feel like a
teenager about to go on his first date. Then in the
afternoon, staff, the Cabinet and I must develop a
plan to handle a potential crisis in the financial
markets; then talk to the American people on
national television about problems we are about to
face. Time to go or I'll be late for rehearsal. I
wonder who the conductor is; does he know the
President is coming to rehearse?*

"Maestro Sullivan, I'm here for rehearsal, where do
you want me?"

"Mr. President, they didn't tell me you were the
singer; I'm pleasantly surprised to say the least."

"Maestro, we better get started, we only have thirty
minutes to rehearse."

"Mr. President, where would you like to stand?"

"If it is okay, I'd like to stand right here, just to the left of the podium; I'll sing following the eulogy."

"Maestro, please have the orchestra play the aria as a warm-up, I'll join you on the second round."

"Not bad Mr. President, but you seem nervous, try to relax and let your voice resonant with the music."

"Maestro let's try it again."

"Much better sir, just let your voice blend with the instruments and you'll do fine."

"I hope so."

Now I better get dressed and pick up the kids, the funeral starts in less than an hour.

"Dad, are you okay, you seem up tight."
"I suppose I am; I hate funerals not to mention having to deliver the eulogy." I haven't told anyone I'll be singing. They'll be surprised and so will millions, watching on television.

Upon entering the church, ushers escort us to our assigned pew."

"Elizabeth, David, kids we're sitting in the front row; so, I can reach the podium in the shortest amount of time."

As the priest and several other speakers deliver their remarks, I can't help but reflect on the past four days and what has happened. Seven months ago, I was midway through my second and last term as Governor; then the nomination for Vice President, then the confirmation process; then just like that, I'm approved. Never, in my wildest dreams, had I imagined I would one day be President. When President Leonard's term ended, I intended to retire from public life. Now here I am, about to deliver a eulogy and perform an aria in front of millions of people.

The First Lady, Susan Leonard, is now walking up to the podium, she's about to introduce me.

"Mr. President, please."

I take a moment to collect my thoughts.

"Today is one of the saddest days of my life. I lost my best friend. Sue Leonard lost her husband. Kate and Jon their Dad, the nation it's President. Today we grieve as a family, death has come.

In the midst of our grief, it's important to remember who he was, his weaknesses and his strengths. Yes, at times he could be difficult. Yet at other times, he was very compassionate. He could laugh with the best, and laugh at himself as well. For me Andrew Leonard was more than a President, he was one of the finest human beings I've ever known.

There are numerous stories I could share with you, but one in particular best describes the man at his best. It shows his willingness to set aside personal safety in order to help another person.

This story took place on July 14, 2011 in Wichita Kansas. Governor Leonard and I were attending a Governor's Conference there. Only two days before, we met for the first time, and we hit it off immediately. During the afternoon break, he and I went outside for some air. It was a beautiful day, not a cloud in the sky, the temperature a moderate eighty-three degrees. After ten minutes or so of casual conversation, the Governor said he wanted to go across the street and visit his favorite ice cream shop. He offered to buy me a cone but I declined.

The street the Governor was about cross was no ordinary street, some six lanes wide at grade, a main thoroughfare. There were stop lights, so I wasn't concerned about his safety; he had made the crossing many times. Once he got across, I turned my attention elsewhere. Probably five minutes later the sound of a loud motorcycle got my attention. As I glanced toward the street, I could see it was traveling at a high rate of speed. If the traffic light nearby, suddenly turned red, there was no way the bike could stop in time. At the same moment I saw what appeared to be an elderly lady about to push the walk button at the same light; she wasn't paying attention to the approaching motorcycle. In a flash, the light turns green and she immediately steps off the curb. Just then, I see Governor Leonard running out of a shop door; he's headed straight towards the old woman, ice cream cone in hand, arms swinging wildly. In an instance, he hooks his arm around her waist and pulls her out of the path of the oncoming cycle. The biker just keeps on going.

The Governor then takes the woman to a nearby bench and sits her down. Soon after a car comes by and picks her up. The Governor then walks back across the street to where I'm sitting. Do you know what he said when he got there? "I lost a great ice cream cone." Nothing else was said. When I asked him what he just did all he says was, "… no big deal, anyone would've done the same thing, now let's get inside."

"The Governor likely saved the old woman's life, and all he had to say was, "I lost a good ice cream cone." That was Andy. From that day on, I never once questioned his motive for doing something.

The President never consider himself, a hero; I'm sure that woman thought otherwise. He is a hero, a person of strength, and humility. That's who Andrew Leonard was. People like him don't come around every day and all too often, we take them for granted. It's only when they are gone, we truly realize how much they contributed. President Leonard contributed a great deal, as a Mayor, as a Governor, as President of the United States; a citizen for the time. Let it be said, he contributed far more than he ever got in return.

Andrew Leonard, our President, Andrew Leonard, my friend. Andy, rest in peace. You are now in God's hands. The American poet Walt Whitman summed it up best.

When lilacs last in the dooryard bloomed
And the great star early drooped in the western sky
in the night, I mourned, and yet shall mourn with
ever returning spring.

Pray for him, pray for his family. His body is gone,
his soul lives on. We'll not forget you." Andy made
a difference

*As I spoke those words, I felt a lump in my throat;
my grief surreal, but near the end, a warmth came
over me; my body suddenly calm; as if God placed
his hand on me and whispered, son it is going to be
all right.*

Thereafter I move forward and to the left of the
podium and await the orchestra. The words to Ava
Maria appear in my mind as if written down.

Ave Maria, gratia plena.

Maria, gratia plena

Maria, gratia plena

Ave, ave dominus,

Dominus tecum.

Benedicta tu in mulieribus,

Et benedictus

Et benedictus fructus ventris,

Ventris tui, Jesus.

Ave Maria.

Sancta Maria,

Ora pro nobis,

Nobis peccatoribus,

Nunc et in hora

Mortis nostrae.

Ave Maria

*As the final notes resonated, the audience appears
trance like, they're quiet and motionless. Did I let
them down, had I embarrassed myself, embarrassed
my family, and most of all the President's family?
The short trip to my seat seemed to take forever;
I'm in shock. When I sit down, Elizabeth looks at
me with that endearing smile of hers; she then gives
gave me a hug. Dad you were wonderful, I had to
hold back tears; it was so moving. Then I turned
around and looked at my son, he to, nodded his
approval. This was the first time a sitting President*

sang to a live audience, in Latin no less. I think it was a success, but tonight I must deliver a different kind of message.

Upon leaving church, I see the President's casket being loaded into a hearse for his final journey home, to Kansas, for burial, I won't be going.

Now look at the time; it's nearly 12:30. That important strategy session starts in less than hour, but first I need to set-up a meeting with Congressional leaders for in the day.

Upon entering the White House, there is Mrs. Witt talking to the Attorney General, which is a bit odd. As I walk towards them, the Attorney General departs quite hurriedly.

"Mrs. Witt, what did the Attorney General want?"

"He said he had new information about Richard."

"Really, so what else did he say?"

"I don't know what you mean."

"We'll talk later, get the Speaker of the House on the phone, I'm going to the Situation Room and don't want to be disturbed once I'm on the phone"

As I closed the door, I couldn't help but think those two are up to something. I never did trust lawyers; maybe it's time for some new people; ones I trust.

Mr. Speaker, how are you?"

"Okay I guess."

"I'll get right to the point, I need to talk to the Congressional leaders this afternoon, say 4:30." "Can it wait" "No Mr. Speaker it can't wait; I have to go now, I'll see you then, good day."

That fellow is a hand full, literally and figuratively. Both parties can bicker all they want; but damm, on this subject they need to work together, we have no choice. The last thing we need is politics as usual.

It's already 1:00; I best write down what I want to discuss at the meeting. When it comes to analytical writing, summary conclusions are the most difficult. I also need to check and make sure the satellite system is up and running.

"Everyone please come in; let's get started. First, the good news, the situation down south has lessened based on the latest information we received. A quake is still likely, although smaller than predicted. I wish I could say the same for the Middle East. Dr. O'Brien, are you there?"

"Yes sir, I'm standing by." "Bill, what's the latest?" "Mr. President, an 8.1 earthquake will likely strike southeast Missouri and northeast Arkansas sometime tomorrow, either late afternoon or early evening, with expected damage, moderate to moderately severe."

"Let me call in the governors and get their assessment. Men, can you hear me?"

"Mr. President, Len Murray, the other governors are here with me."

"Len what's your level of readiness?"

"Sir all participating agencies are standing by, ready to assist as needed. This evening the others governors and I will hold a news conference to release our plan for dealing with the situation."

"Len, do you and the other governors need anything more from me?"

"For now, we're good to go Mr. President; the Secretary of Homeland Security is also standing by if we need him."

"Len that's great to hear. Fellows, stay with us, now we're going to talk about the Middle East."

"Dr. O'Brien, please bring us up to date, where do things stand right now?"

"Mr. President, sir, worse than we thought, let me use a model to illustrate what I'm talking about. We now think the quake will start here, approximately 30 miles south southeast of Yalta in the Black Sea, along the border of Turkey and Iraq. Its path will then move southward along the Tigris River into the Persian Gulf, approximately twenty-five miles off the Iraq coast then cross over the northeast coast of United Arab Emirates into the Gulf of Oman then head almost due east to Karchi, Pakistan, and finally diminishing in intensity as it enters India. As I mentioned before, this quake will start well below the surface, and produce a tremendous amount of energy. Throughout the region, massive upheavals in the earth will occur, potentially destroying underground oil supplies. Tidal waves and wide spread flooding will also take place in an area one hundred and fifty miles either side of the fault centerline. We also think the quake will last about thirty to forty minutes; aftershocks however will likely go on for two to three hours, followed by more aftershocks for another thirty days. I'm not an economist, but a quake of this magnitude, possibly 9.7, will likely affect financial markets."

"Dr. O'Brien, Admiral Timm how many casualties might they have."

"Sir, it could be in the tens of thousands, maybe more; injuries, ten times that. Understand, these are estimates, nobody really knows the true extent, remember it has been 150,000 years since we had a quake this big."

"Mr. President."

"Thanks, Bill." "Folks, this event will have a major impact on our future. The financial fallout could be tremendous, not to mention the loss of lives and damage to property. Our way of life could change, at least in some fashion. The thought, truly unnerves me. As such we must protect our interests in the best way we know how. I would like to hear your thoughts. Admiral Timm."

"Mr. President, what should we do with our military forces and their equipment?"

"Admiral, I just prepared a directive ordering all personnel, ships, and aircraft be recalled from the affected area. In addition, Plan Alpha 2-B shall be implemented for all equipment left behind. In fact, I want you to personally initiate that directive, including Alpha 2-B."

"Sir, I'm on it." "Admiral I want you back here when you're finished handling it."
"Secretary Coles, what about the financial community, I want to hear your thoughts."

"Mr. President, I think the first thing we need to do is suspend Wall Street trading, beginning tomorrow."

"Mr. Secretary how long should it be suspended?"
"Mr. President, five business days sounds like a safe number, maybe longer, if necessary."

"What do we do about overseas assets; anyone have any ideas, anyone. Should we recall them?"

"Mr. President." "Secretary Williams."
"Sir, won't that cause a panic?"

"Bob, in all probability, there will be a panic any way. The book value of all assets, in this country and around the world, will likely take a hit, possibly as high as thirty percent. The one thing we can count on is instability. Therefore, it's important we try to contain it to the greatest extent possible. Panic creates more panic; usually making matters worse than they really are. We need to project confidence; it will get better, even though we will suffer setbacks along the way. Speaking of time, what about our energy supplies. How long might our oil reserves last?"

"Secretary Johnson, what is you guess?"
"Mr. President, we now have a 180-day supply of crude oil, a 90-day supply of refined gasoline and diesel fuel, and an unlimited supply of natural gas."

"How much gasoline do we currently export?"

"Right now about 1.2 billion gallons per day."

"Ray, we'll need every bit of that. Therefore, I'm issuing a directive the will suspend all gasoline exports until further notice; whether by ship or pipeline. The directive won't apply to exports now loaded aboard ships that are about to sail."

"People, how will the international community react to our decisions? Madam Secretary."

"Sir, there'll be chaos throughout the Middle East, and likely we'll be blame for it."

"What should we do?"

"I don't think anybody knows right now."

"What about the Russians, will they try something given the circumstances, and how about the Chinese."

"Mr. President I wish I had the answer."

"Martin, how is the media going to react, here and overseas?"

"Sir, they'll be just as confused as we are."

"Folks, the next few days, maybe the next few weeks will be very unpredictable. As a nation we will be severely tested; and the outcome uncertain."

"The strategy we choose will require commitments from everyone, to succeed in the long term. If any of you want out or are not committed, tell me now or after the meeting. This country must speak with one voice, mine. I know I was appointed to this job; by events beyond my control. Nevertheless, I have a job to do, and I'm going to do everything possible to be successful at it. I expect each of you to do your best as well. We will get through this, but only if we take the challenge head on. I want all of you to prepare an analysis of your department's readiness, to meet the challenges we are about to face. Based on the most recent data, those quakes will likely occur within the next sixty hours. Time is critical; we'll reconvene again immediately after the first event occurs. Are there any questions? No, then let's get to it."

"Martin, let me see the draft of my speech."

"Mr. President, I must apologize, I haven't gotten very far."

"Well let me see it; Martin I must say I'm disappointed. What have you been working on the past few hours, it certainly isn't this."

"Sir, this thing spooks me; call it writer's block."

"Have you arranged airtime?"

"No, because I didn't think I'd have the speech ready in time."

"You may be right; schedule it for tomorrow night, same time. Call me when it's set. By the way, who is the best writer in your department?"

"That would be Kris Renstrom." "Is she good, what's her background?"

"Sir, she's an excellent writer and has an advanced in journalism. I can send you her resume and references if you wish".

"Please do; then have her come to my office."

Now I must call the kids.

"David is Elizabeth and the kids with you?"

"Yes, Dad they are."

"Good; I want everyone to come to the White House for dinner, be here at 6:00, and call your Aunt and tell her to come."
"I will Dad." Okay, see you then."

Now, time to relax before the brain trust gets here.
"Mr. President, the Congressional leaders are here."
"Okay, give me a minute then show them in."

"Good afternoon everyone; thanks for coming. I wish it were under more pleasant circumstances. By now, most of you have heard about the earthquakes, here and in the Middle East. The latest information suggests ours will be less severe than first thought. Scientists now think it'll be less than 7.2. Nevertheless, we must prepare plans for a worst case; the plan must include medical and National Guard personnel. The Secretary of Homeland Security will coordinate things with area governors. The Middle East situation, is far more serious."

Let me replay Bill O'Brien's presentation, it explains it better than I can. Let me warn you, it's quite horrific.

Looking around the room, I see startled faces everywhere, everyone is speechless.

"Mr. President, what are we going to do? This will send shock waves through the financial community."

"You're right Senator Roth."

"Tomorrow I plan to speak to the American people on this very subject and outline possible scenarios. Everyone will have to work together, the American people, the business community, and most importantly the elected officials to resolve the situation. Now is not the time to grandstand, gamesmanship or backdoor wheeling and dealing."

"The plan I'm proposing contains three critical elements. First, I will suspend Wall Street trading for five days, longer if necessary. Second, I will order a halt to all gasoline exports, whether by pipeline or tanker. Ships loaded prior to issuance will be allowed to leave. Third, overseas financial assets owned by the United States and/or chartered American businesses will be recalled, to the full extent possible."

"As circumstances become more evident following the quake, I'll make the appropriate adjustments. People, if we mess this up, the way we do business may change forever. It's our job to lessen the impact these quakes might have, if that's possible; if ever there was a time to step-up, it's now. Can I count on your help? Mr. Speaker."

"Sir, what can we do?" I'd like you to appoint four people, one from each party in the House and the Senate. They will serve on a special Presidential Commission, authorized by Executive Order 031618-02. The Commissioners will work with me and the Cabinet on mitigating the crisis. Mr. Speaker, Senator Roth, can we get this done? Senator Roth."

"Yes, Mr. President we can."

"Men, once the Commission is formed all the communications between Congress and the White House will be handled by that body. That's all I have; I'm going to have dinner with my family. I suggest you do the same. Mr. Speaker, can I talk to you alone?"

"If possible, I want you on that Commission."

"Sir, the House must decide that."

"I know, but I can use your expertise."

"Mr. President we'll see what happens."
"Oh by the way, your performance at the President's funeral was outstanding. Where did you learn to sing like that?"

"Thanks Mr. Speaker, I picked it up along the way."

"Mrs. Witt, can you come in here? Have a seat; I need to talk to you."

"Sir, what's this about?"

"Your little chat with the Attorney General worries me. Is there anything you'd like to tell me?"

"No, not really, at least nothing I can think."

"Mrs. Witt, if we're going to work together, we have to trust each other. Nothing troubles me more than having people sneaking around behind my back or not doing what they are suppose to do.. Let me be perfectly clear; I have no patience for that kind of behavior. I know we've only worked together for a short while, and with everything that has happened, we've had no time to talk. Now that you know where I stand, do you still want to stay?"

"Yes Mr. President I do.

Okay then, you can go; let me know when my family gets here."

I know what she said, but I'm not sure I believe her; maybe a change is needed.

"Kids, Lynn, come in, let's talk; dinner won't be ready for another twenty minutes. Susie, Jack, what did you kids do this afternoon?"

"Grandpa, Mom and Uncle David took us to the zoo; we watched the animals play; we even petted the elephants."

"Dad they really had a good time." "David, how are you getting along?"

"Pop, I should be asking you that question."

"What I mean is how is school going; have you started your thesis?"

"It's rough but I'm surviving, and I plan to start writing next month."

"Have you picked a title?"

"Yes, "Living in the 22nd Century Economy."

"Sound interesting, has it been preapproved?"
"They're considering it; I should know next week."
"What are your plans; is everyone going home tomorrow?"

"Yes Dad, our plane leaves at 9:30; the kids have school, David and I have to get back to work."

"Lynn, how was your day?"

"Productive but challenging; and we need to talk."

"You can plan on it, just not right now. Let's all sit, the food is ready; kids I asked the chef to fix your favorite—cheese pizza."

"Dad, thanks for a great meal; we have to go, the kids have to get a good night's sleep, and you should get one to."

"Your right Elizabeth I hope to; now everyone, give me a hug; I love you guys. Have a good trip; I'll call you tomorrow evening. Lynn, sit down, would you like a drink?"

"Love one."

"So, tell me did you find anything new regard Andy's health?"

"Yes, I did. It seems the President had a very rare blood disorder, it was discovered during his last physical. If the condition, left untreated, would lead to complications, specifically compromise his immune system."

"Was he getting treatment?" "No, and that's the strange part."

"When I asked Boardman why, he said he didn't think it was necessary. That really bothered me; drugs for treating it have been available for years, yet the President's own doctor chose not to prescribe them. I also asked the good doctor if he told the President about his condition. He said "no, I don't think so". Then I got even madder, so mad I nearly strangled him—I didn't; you know the man is an idiot."

"Lynn, do you think it played a role in his death?" "It could have, but I have to run some more tests when I get home."

"Can't you do it here?"

"No, I don't have the equipment I need, and if I ask for it, it could raise questions."

"So, when are you leaving?"

"My plane leaves at 10:00 tomorrow morning."

"Lynn, we should stop now, I need time to relax and unwind?"

"Certainly, I do to.

"Madam, could I fix you another drink?" "Yes."

"John, come sit down next to me. Now isn't this nice? How are you holding up?"

"Okay I guess, although it's probably a little too early to tell. When the earthquake hits the Middle East, all hell is going to break lose."
"Is it that serious?"

"Yes."

"What about the quake in Missouri, is that looking bad to?"

"Thankful no, the seismic activity has diminished considerably in the past day."

"What's it like being President?"

"Having the job, given everything that has occurred, trying, but I'm managing."

"Stressful I suppose."

"Lynn you don't know the half of it."

"Stand up John, let me rub your shoulders, it'll help you relax."

"Oh, that feels great, now if we could do something about my back."

"Lie down; I'll do what I can. How does that feel?"

"It feels fantastic."

Then, without saying a word, she rolls me over on my side lies down next to me and snuggles in. I admit I haven't felt this good in a long time. Now she's rubbing my stomach, then my hips and upper thighs; it's relaxing but also unsettling.

"Lynn, be careful or this might lead to something we aren't prepared for."

"Mr. President, not to worry."

"Lynn, we should probably call it a night."

"Okay, if you wish."

Lynn is an attractive woman and hard to ignore.

"John, I'm going now, I have reading to do."

"Lynn so do I. Call me in the morning before your flight leaves."

"I can do that; by the way, you have a great smile."

"Yes, I put it to use every now and then."

Day Six

Tuesday March 5 2:45 am

After hours of tossing and turning, now the phone.

"Mr. President."

"Yes, what is it?"

"Sir, the quake in the Middle East has started; ours could start within the hour, or possibly two."

"Wayne, get a hold of the Cabinet, staff, and Admiral Timm, and have them meet me in the Situation Room in thirty minutes. Also, tell Secretary Johnson to have the satellite feed up and running as soon as possible."

I'm thinking, is this for real or is it a dream. Maybe a warm shower will clear my head; it feels good. I can't stop thinking about the next few days, so many decisions. I must stay ahead of things, less they get out of hand, which may happen anyway.

"Good morning everyone; let's get started we have lots of work to do. Ray, is the satellite feed up and running?"

"Yes, sir it is, we have Dr. O'Brien standing by."

"Bill if you hear me give me a quick update, start with our quake."

"Mr. President, moderate eruptions are now occurring in sections of Missouri, about 105 miles south southeast of St. Louis."

"Bill, how bad will it get?"

"We have good news to report; we now believe the quake will not exceed 7.2, and most of the urban area, mostly minor damage. However, there'll be major flooding on the Mississippi River, how much we don't know, perhaps seven to eight feet over flood stage, maybe more. Casualties, we think, will be light, depending on the number of aftershocks. Injuries will also be less than predicted; livestock won't fare as well, due to flooding. Mr. President."

"Secretary Johnson, are all the items the governors requested ready to go?"

"Yes sir, everything is set; I just double checked before I came."

"Bill, tell us about the Middle East."

"That quake, which began in earnest about thirty minutes ago, is huge, larger in scope than we first thought. However, we did accurately predict the centerline of the quake and its subsequent path; what we underestimated was the width of the impact zone. Instead of ten to fifteen miles we had forecast, the actual width will be closer to fifty. In addition, we now know shipping lanes were altered, and some may no longer be usable in the future. Also, the tsunami waves could reach a height of seventy-five feet in some areas. As for casualties and injuries, I won't venture a guess, but they could be massive. When it's all over, I'm afraid the region won't be the same. Mr. President."

"Okay everyone, from now on, things get tricky. As I said yesterday, we simply can't sit back and do nothing. Financial markets will likely go crazy; and dammed if I'm going to let that happen. The oil industry is also going to be another trouble spot; they'll try to capitalize on the situation; and I can't allow that to happen. The decisions we must make must be done quickly, and in the best interests of the country, even if they upset some people, and they will. The first thing I want to talk about is Wall Street."

"Secretary Coles, what do you think the Federal Reserve's position will be?"

"Mr. President, they won't support us."
"What would they propose as an alternative; sit back and watch everything fall apart? Mr. Secretary, we don't have the luxury of sitting around until they think up a solution. What do the rest of 'you' people think? Roberts, your thoughts."

"I agree with you, we just can't wait around, by then it'll be too late. Suspending trading will give us time to prepare for the long haul, and sir we also might have to suspend bank transfers, at least internationally, for a time." "Thank you, Wayne."

"Has anyone talked to the European Union or International Monetary Fund? Secretary Coles."

"Mr. President, I placed a call to each of them, but I haven't heard back."

"Mr. Edwards, how is the media going to react to our choices; will they stand with us or might they turn this into a theatrical production?"
"To be frank sir, I don't know. I think we should appeal to their sense of duty, to do what is good for the country, and not turn this into a circus."

"Secretary Conrad how will the international community react to our decisions?"

"Sir, I'm sure our enemies will denounce us, at least publicly, behind the scenes they'll keep asking for assistance. I'll support whatever decision(s) you make; this is all new to us, there's no precedence."

"Secretary Williams, Admiral Timm, what are your fellow's take on this. Mr. Secretary."

"Sir, in the short term, the military won't be involved, but in the long term, we may be called upon to maintain order in certain places. I think you must make decisions which are right for the country; I know the men and women of the armed forces will support you completely."

"Admiral Timm."

"I agree with the Secretary's assessment. We probably have to write the rules as we go; this is new ground for everyone."

"Admiral, did we get all the troops and equipment out of there?"

"Sir, all ships are safely out, but we couldn't evacuate all of our personnel; close to seven hundred remain in the area. We couldn't round up enough planes in the allotted time period to evacuate everyone. We also had to leave numerous pieces of equipment behind. However, we did manage to destroy all the data and classified equipment before we pulled out."

"Admiral thank you, now we need to focus our attention on the oil situation."

"I'd like to ask each of you, what do you think the long-term impact might be and will it be permanent. Let's start with the Energy. Mr. Secretary."
"Mr. President, I think our way of life, as we know it will be changed forever, if we lose Middle East oil. Even if there isn't a prolonged disruption, we'll still experience major shortages. The price of crude oil, likely, could triple or quadruple in the short term; this will cause production delays and cutbacks, and most certainly job losses."

"Treasury Secretary Coles could you give us a broader assessment of the financial market, what would you suggest? Sir the first thing I'd do, freeze oil, gasoline, and natural gas prices, effective immediately or until such time as we can assess the impacts from the quake. I understand you've discussed the idea of suspending Wall Street trades, be it briefly; and I support that. Next, I suggest we ask businesses and individuals in this country to cut back on the amount of oil and gasoline they consume. I know that might be a stretch, but we have to try. Finally, I suggest we reaffirm our relationship with Canada; after all, they're our largest supplier of crude oil."

"Mr. Secretary, how would you feel if we halt gasoline exports, at least in interim?"

"Mr. President, I think everything has been put on the table."

"Thank you."

"What about our military and defense capabilities; Mr. Defense Secretary, can we effectively operate with less oil?"

"Sir, I don't know the answer to that, but what I do know, our men and women will come up with a solution for handling the shortage. I estimate military oil reserves could last four months, maybe five if we conserve prudently. My guess is, we can get by near term, it's the long term that concerns me the most." Let's take a short break."

After listening to these people for over an hour, I can see why they're as bewildered and troubled as I am. I think I have some of the answers; I don't like most of them, but times have changed. The toughest part is convincing everyone else, that we as a nation, we must take such steps, but that's the job of the President isn't it? As Truman might say, thousands could do a better job than me, but I'm stuck with it, and by golly I'm going to do it and do it the best I can and that's that. "Okay folks, back to work. Mr. Edwards, how do you think the public will react?"

"Mr. President, they'll be in stunned, and they'll assume the worst. Losing a job, losing some or most of their financial resources, or knowing their way of life will change; will scare the hell out of them. They'll want to blame someone, and the media could play on that. I'm sorry to say, I don't have an answer for any of it. Maybe if we could convince the media it's in their best interests to work with us, instead of playing the blame game. Somehow, we must convince them they have a stake in all of this, it might make a difference. It's certainly worth a try."

"I agree Mr. Edwards. My high school softball coach used to say, if you can't catch the ball, at least knock it down and keep it in front of you. I think the axiom certainly applies. Mr. Speaker, we haven't heard from you; what's your take?"

"Mr. President, Congress worries that some of your proposals might cause irreparable harm." "Well, does the Congress think I should sit back and do nothing and let things take their course?"

"No." "Well then, what do they propose?"
"I need time to talk it over with the other members before I can offer any recommendations."

"Mr. Speaker, time is not on our side; we/I have to make some tough decisions now. The last thing we need is for your people to sit back and point fingers and blame everyone else; if that's the only thing that happens, then prepare for the worst. Speaker Campbell, Senator Roth, as leaders of your respective chambers it's time for you to step-up. If we delay, our ability to control what might happen might be lost forever. I'm sure you don't want that; I certainly don't think anyone in this room does. Do I have your backing?"

"Sir, in light of the situation, you do."

"Thank you." "Mr. George, Mr. Roberts, I haven't heard from you, do you have anything to say?" "Mr. President, from a legal perspective, I don't think you have the authority to implement these measures."

"What bothers you the most, the possibility a President, takes drastic measures or the possibility of having to defend a lawsuit?"

"Sir, I don't know how to answer that."

"Well Mr. George, let me tell you what would happen if we do nothing. First, there'll be mass selling on Wall Street; individual and corporate investment plans could lose up to fifty percent of their value. Second, there might be a run on the banks and/or banks may demand immediate and full repayment on personal and business loans; those that don't pay, would find themselves in default. Finally, we could see the price of oil and gas double or triple the first day; and big oil will likely hoard supplies. So Mr. George, how would you handle those situations? Not sure, I'd rather catch hell for doing something than for doing nothing."
"I see your point."

"Mr. Roberts, anything to add?"

"No, I think everything that should be said was."

"Okay, let me summarize the tenets of Executive Order 030618. Effective immediately, all Wall Street trading will be suspended for five days, and if necessary suspended further, in three day segments and/or until such time the financial situation has stabilized. Second, gas and oil prices including natural gas, shall be locked in at their current price, as of 12:01 am this day. In addition, all exports of refined gasoline, aviation fuel and natural and LP gas are frozen at their current price, until further notice. Finally, all international banking activity, involving transfers shall cease, less items provided in the Addendum, until further notice."

People, these are tough measures but necessary ones. Right now, we don't know the full extent of damage in the Middle East, and we won't for at least a few days, maybe longer. When new information becomes available, I'll make the necessary changes."

"Mr. President, Dr. O'Brien wants to join us via satellite; he has some updates."

"Bill, are you there?"

"Yes Mr. President I am." "What do you have?"

"Sir, here is the good news. The earthquake here caused only moderately severe damage. Older structures were hit the hardest; in the rural areas inland flooding generates most of the destruction, but livestock generally spared. Right now, we do not have a precise count on injuries or deaths, but early reports suggest the death total is less than two hundred, injuries could have been four or five hundred. Overall, the emergency response has been excellent, based on reports from the field commanders. Also, the primary shock is over, although aftershocks will go on for several weeks; with minimal impact; and that's good news."

"Bill; what's the situation in the Middle East?"

"Sir, that quake appears stronger than we anticipated; the largest reading so far, 9.7. The primary shock should end within the hour, having run the full length, as predicted, to the western border of Pakistan. The quake also generated a large tidal wave. Unfortunately, we don't know the status of underground oil supplies; we can only hope for the best. Finally, we have no solid information concerning deaths or injuries; but we assume it's large. It will take some time before we know anything concrete."

"Thanks Bill; unless someone has anything new, I'm going to adjourn the meeting. Mr. George, Mr. Coles, please stay we need to talk. Mr. Edwards, schedule a press briefing for 8:30."

"Mr. George, I want you to prepare a final draft of my Executive Order, have it ready for my signature prior to the briefing. I'll sign it at the conclusion of my remarks. Do you have questions?"

"No sir, I don't."

"Mr. Coles, I need you to get in touch with the Chairman of the New York Stock Exchange and inform him of my Executive Order. I also want you to contact the Chairman of the Federal Reserve and let him know I'm suspending trading, effective immediately. If he gives you any trouble have him call me. Let's get to work; I need to prepare for the press briefing."

Isn't this great, I've been President less than a week; buried Andrew Leonard, experienced two earthquakes, one with serious consequences; and now my first press briefing. Can it get more interesting, I certainly hope not? Now where did I leave my laptop, oh there it is. What to say at the briefing; I think my comments should be brief, and to the point. In addition, I think it's a good idea to limit Q&A, possibly to ten questions or less. Now time to write it down; best leave time for review.

"Martin, what is?"

"Mr. President, we need to go."

"Let's chat on the way."

"Martin I'm going to open with some general comments; that should last no more than three to four minutes; following that, I'll open it up for questions. Please announce in advance, time for questions will be limited; I don't want the briefing turning into a debate. Clear?"

"Yes, very clear, by the way look, out for that UPI reporter, he's a troublemaker."

"Thanks."

"Mr. President, here is your Executive Order; you may wish to read it before you go in." "Thanks Frank. Martin, give me a minute. Frank it looks fine; after I sign it, don't forget to affix the Presidential seal before making copies." "I won't sir." "Martin, I'm right behind you."

"Please be seated, I have one announcement before the President comes out; we only have time for a few questions following the President's remarks; now the President of the United States."

"Thank you all for coming on such short notice; events in the Middle East and here in this country have made this briefing necessary. I'd like to start with a brief overview of how things now stand; then I'll take questions."

"For the past week, scientists and geologists have been watching seismic activity here and in the Middle East. Early last evening a large 7.1 earthquake occurred along the borders of Kentucky, Missouri, Tennessee, and Arkansas. Fortunately, the quake wasn't as big as scientists first thought, and so far, no deaths have been reported, and injuries are much smaller than first believed. Property damage however, was rather extensive. Homeland Security, the Department of Defense, the area governors and I, started preparing for this event several days ago, and all reports now indicate that preparation paid off. I wish that were the case in the Middle East."

"At approximately 2:25 AM, Eastern Standard Time, a quake in excess of 9.2 occurred in southwest Russia, near the northeastern corner of the Black Sea. This event triggered a succession of quakes along the eastern end of the Black Sea, stretching down through the Persian Gulf and the Gulf of Oman before reaching the western border of Pakistan. All of this took place less than an hour. Since that time, there have been numerous reports of aftershocks. Seismologists have told us these aftershocks could go on for weeks. So far, I haven't received a report on deaths or injuries. Recent satellite data indicates major shifts in the earth surface, generating tidal waves, and causing extensive structural damage in Iraq, Iran, Syria, and United Arab Emirates. Once the area is stable, we're prepared to assist the affected countries, if asked to do so. So far, no assistance has been requested." Given the enormity of the event, and its potential consequences for the United States, I've issued, with the concurrence of the Congress and the Cabinet, Executive Order 030618. As follows, here are the provisions: effectively immediately, all Wall Street trading will be suspended for five days, and if necessary suspended further, in three-day increments and/or until such time the financial situation has stabilized. Next, I've frozen the price of gasoline, oil and natural gas at their current price levels, as of 12:01 am this day. In addition, I've suspended all exports of refined gasoline, aviation fuel and natural and LP gas, until further notice. Finally, I've suspended, until further notice, all overseas bank transactions that involve transfers with other countries, except those provided for in Addendum A of the order. I know these are tough measures, but they are necessary; given we won't know the full extent of the destruction in the Middle East for days, perhaps months. As such, we needed time to prepare short and long-term plans once that information becomes available; if adjustments are necessary they will be made accordingly.

Now I'll take your questions."

"Mr. President, Sam Anders, NBC News. Sir, why did you take this action now? Shouldn't we wait to see what happens?"

"Sam, I have a good idea what will happen if I sat back and waited. First, there would be massive selling on Wall Street, creating a near panic environment. Second, we would likely see the price of crude oil and gasoline double, maybe triple, almost immediately. In addition, hoarding would likely occur. Finally, major investors and other private entities, and possibly individuals, might make a run on the banks; if any of those events took place, nothing could stop them. My Order buys us time. Who has the next question?"

"Mr. President, Lynne Rodgers, Newsweek. Was there an autopsy performed on President Keller, and if so when will we know the results?"

"Yes, an autopsy was performed on the President, but we don't have those results yet. When we do we'll announce them; I hope by next week."

"Sir, was foul play involved in his death?

"I've no information to that effect."

"Mr. President, Bill Stewart, Fox News. Sir, I heard you haven't been sleeping well these past few nights, is that true?"

"Thank you for your concern Mr. Stewart. Let me answer that by asking you a question. How well would you sleep if you were waking up at 3:45 and told the President is dead, and you'll now assume the office of the President of the United within the hour? Then several days later you were told that two major earthquakes would likely strike within the next few days. Then at 3:30 this morning you were wakened to news that a massive quake did occur in the Middle East, the impact of which will have major consequences for the Unites States."

"Sir, I get your point."

"Mr. President, we have time for one more question."

"Sir, Betty Norman, Hard News. Who was the woman sleeping at the White House the night before, an old acquaintance perhaps?"

"Madam, I shouldn't dignify that remark with a response, but I will any way. The woman in question is my sister-in-law, the younger sister of my late wife, who also happens to be a very good doctor; she was here at my request to assist with the autopsy of President Keller, and yes, she did stay in the White House. Where I come from, relatives who are invited into our home aren't asked to stay in a in a hotel for the night. Now thank all of you for coming, the Press Secretary will hold additional briefings as the need arises."

"Mr. President, I'm sorry about that I should've warned you about her." "Martin it's okay."

"Mr. Roberts, get the southern governors on the phone, I need to speak to them; but first I need some fresh air." I motion to my Secret Service agent that I'm going outside. He quickly heads my way.

"Sir, are you planning to take a walk?"

"Yes, and a few laps around the Rose Garden."

I knew it was too good to last, I see the Treasury
Secretary running towards me waving his arm.
"Mr. President, the Chairman of the New York
Stock Exchange called and wants to speak to you
right away." Is he upset? "You might say that."

"Good, those folks need to come down to earth on
occasion. Well go ahead, get him on the phone, I'll
be back in the Oval Office directly. I know what
he'll say, Mr. President you can't suspend trading."

"Mr. Andersen, what can I do for you?"

"Mr. President, you can't just suspend trading."

"Sir, yes I can. I'm not going to sit back and watch
a major selloff, let speculation skyrocket, and go
through the roof. That hurts everyone, except your
traders. Protecting this country from financial ruin
is my top priority; it should be yours as well;

everyone needs to step back and take a deep breath. I think the next couple of days will give us a clearer picture of what we have to deal with; then we can implement more precise strategies for handling the situation. We'll get through this."

"Okay Mr. President." "Good day Mr. Andersen."

He's probably cursing me now, but I don't care.

"Mrs. Witt, is the link with the governors in place yet?" "Sir, it should be ready in a minute." "Fellows, how are things?"

"Mr. President, Len Murray, things are going much better than we expected. I can't speak for the other governors, but I can say all the advanced planning certainly paid off."

"Did the Homeland Secretary do his job; did he get medical personnel and equipment rounded up in a timely manner?"

"Tom Petersen.

"Mr. President, he certainly did."

"How do the injury and death reports look?"

"As far as we know, about twenty people are dead; two to three hundred are injured."

"What about property damage, any data yet?"

"Sir, its Len. The rural and low-lying areas appear to be hit the hardest. A goodly number of roads and bridges are destroyed; however, we don't know the full extent of damage, but we believe it could prove moderate. We're continuing to monitor."

"Men, that sounds good, if things go as planned, I hope to fly down and inspect the area tomorrow. If you like, we could meet in Memphis, and discuss the next step; then I'd like do a fly over."

"Mr. President, Tom here; sounds good."

"You men are doing a great job; keep it up."

"Mr. President, I hate to interrupt, but your sister-in-law is on the phone and she said it's urgent. Do you want to talk to her?"

"Yes, Mrs. Witt; fellows I have to hang up, I'll see you tomorrow."

"Hi Lynn, what's up?"

"John, I just finished my lab analysis, and the news is not good, I even ran the tests several times to reconfirm my findings."
"What do they show?"

"They show the bacteria we found in the President's body coupled with his medical condition likely made his heart stop beating." "Are you sure?"

"Yes I am. The one thing I don't know, how he contracted the bacteria in the first place."

"Lynn, I asked the Attorney General to review the President's appointment schedule for the last seventy-two hours, up to the time he went to bed."

"John, are you certain you can trust him?"

"Lynn, why do you ask?"

"When he accompanied me to Dr. Boardman's office, he kept asking me all kinds of questions, the kind a layperson would not typically ask; and that's what made me suspicious. How well do you know him; is he trustworthy?"

"Lynn, hardly at all, maybe I cannot."

"Have you told anyone else about your findings?"

"No."

"Good, keep it that way. Also, don't leave your lab analysis file on your PC, transfer it to a memory stick, and keep it in a safe place. In addition, after you copy the file, change the data in your analysis file on your PC before deleting it, do it twice."

"John, why is that so important?"

"Lynn, whenever you change data in a file most programs generate a backup file before saving the file that was changed. By doing it twice, you eliminate any chance of restoring the first backup file; that's the one containing your findings."

"Okay I'll do that right now."

"Lynn, any time you need to talk, just call."

"John, I'll do that; I'm still confused about what happened the other night." "So am I."

Now I have three things to worry about, the quake in the Middle East, the suspicious nature of the President's death, and now a potentially awkward situation with Lynn. Mother always said there would be days like this.

"Mrs. Witt get Wayne Roberts on the phone; I need to speak to him right away."

"Mr. President, Mr. Roberts is on the line."

"Mr. Roberts." "Call me Wayne."

"Okay Wayne, I need to schedule a flight tomorrow morning; I'm going to Memphis to meet the southern governors. After that, we'll take an aerial tour of the quake sites. We hope to leave Andrews around 9 o'clock."

"Sir, I'll make the arrangements, what about the press corps?"

"For this flight, no more than five, you pick which ones and Wayne no tail gunners. Okay."
Should be an interesting morning, my first trip on Air Force One; with five reporters, all wishing to interview the "new" President but that's tomorrow, I should call Bill O'Brien.

"Bill, what's the latest on the Middle East?"

"Mr. President, good afternoon. As of now, we haven't received any new information on the underground geology or to what extent the quake may have compromised the natural oil supplies. We

144

are however, putting together several models, which could give us a better idea of the situation; those models should be ready in about two hours."

"Bill, let me know as soon as you have them put together." "I certainly will."

"Mr. President, there is one thing we do know; the shipping lanes are now littered with rock formations, all hazardous to shipping. We hope to map them as soon as possible."

"Thanks for the good work; please get back to me as soon as you have them mapped."

I should have the Energy Secretary with me when I view those models, but I'm not certain if I should invite someone from big oil. I know the Chair of Conoco-Phillips is meeting with a congressional subcommittee this afternoon. I suppose, if I invite him, someone from Congress will want to tag along. I should think about that one. Now maybe I can get a little time for myself, even play the piano.

"Mrs. Witt, I'll be in the East Room; come and get me when Dr. O'Brien calls."

Maybe I shouldn't play; it might bother some people. Let me see if I can remember that Chopin piece from memory. I think it's coming to me.

While playing, my mind drifts off into a peaceful dream; I imagine my family is seated beside me, smiling and having a good time, a time preceding the accident. Everything changes after that; I felt alone, the kids had grown and moved away, nothing seemed the same. I remember the last time I held my wife's hand; that memory will never leave, much like loneliness; then a voice.

"John, Mr. President."

I know that voice; it's Sue Leonard.

"Sue I'm sorry I didn't hear you at first, I must have been dreaming."

"John, I know you have a lot on your mind." "What can I do for the First Lady?"

"Mr. President, I wanted to let you know I'm moving out of the White House this afternoon."

"Sue, I thought you were in Kansas." "I was, and planned to stay there after the burial and have my belongings shipped, however, last night I decided to fly back and wrap up a few loose ends; I'll be leaving tonight. Oh by the way, you play beautifully; don't let me interrupt."

"It's okay; I needed time alone before studying reports on the Middle East quake."

"John, has your sister-in-law completed her work on the autopsy?"

"For the most part, but she got called back to work before she could finish. She tells me she can finish what's left from there; shouldn't be more than two or three days. The only thing she is certain of, his death caused, in part, by a mutated strain of rare bacteria; unfortunately, we have no clues how he came in contract with it; and we may never know."

"John, I'm leaving now, would you mind if I give you a hug."

"No not at all, keep in touch. Could you close the door when you leave; thanks." *I should call*

Congressman Peters before it gets too late.

"Congressman Peters, John Keller. Is the Chairman of Conoco/Phillips still with you? He is, good. I'd like both of you to come over, preferably within the hour, to watch a geological presentation of the after effects produced by the Middle East earthquake. I only have one condition; don't discuss the purpose of your visit with anyone; just tell the Chairman that you got invited to the White House to meet the President. I'll explain later. Do I have your assurance?"

"Yes, you have it"

"Great, come to the Situation Room when you arrive; I'll be waiting there. Wayne what is it?"

"Mr. President, turn on the television, a popular conservative and several people from Capitol Hill are about to render political commentary; Ray Rush is the host."

"Good evening ladies and gentlemen, tonight we are going to talk about the President's plan for the country. "The first speaker is Senator Cane, Senator Cane."

"The President's plan, as proposed, will cripple the country, and create financial hardships."

"Senator Cane I agree, the President should've waited until he knew all the facts before taking action. Congressman Carr, what's your opinion."

"Well sir, sitting back and doing nothing would be foolhardy. Fact, we know the quake will affect Middle East oil supplies. Fact, much of the infrastructure in the region will likely be destroyed. Fact, we don't know to what extent underground oil supplies are affected. Fact, if Wall Street continued trading, we would see mass activity and major sell offs, with oil futures probably going thru the roof. That alone, would cause a financial crisis; and if it happens, many Americans could lose thousands of dollars. Fact, if Big Oil elected to hoard gas and oil supplies, which I'm quite sure they would, it would adversely affect all Americans. Gentlemen, we simply can't stand by and allow these things to happen; we need time to sort through the facts and develop sound and effective strategies to get through this crisis, and it is a crisis, make no mistake. What we don't need is a bunch of talking bubbleheads suggesting bad alternatives. Fellows, if you were true Americans, as you claim, you'd support the very people working to solve things."

"Mrs. Witt, call Congressman Carr's office right now and tell them I want to speak to him as soon as possible. Then get me the news directors of Fox,

150

NBC, CBS, and ABC on the phone; I think they are in town for Congressional hearings; make it a conference call. I'll be in the Situation Room, so transfer it there."

I was hoping I wouldn't have to resort to this so soon, but it looks like they forced my hand.

"Mr. President, Congressman Carr is on the line."

"Congressman, I want you to come to the White House and watch a briefing on the geological impact from the Middle East quake, it will start in ninety minutes. Can you make it?" "Yes."

"Good, by the way thanks for setting 'those' people straight. Few issues to challenge them"

I wonder how Mrs. Witt is coming with those news boys. I'm sure they don't get calls from the President every day of the week; they are now.

"Mr. President, all four newsmen are on the line, and standing by." "Thanks Mrs. Witt."

"Men, as you know, the Middle East just experienced a massive earthquake, effecting millions of people and causing wide-spread destruction. In ninety minutes, I'll be watching a presentation on the geological effects from that quake. Several renowned geologists put the presentation together. It's imperative this information is reported to the public, truthfully and accurately. That's why I want each of you here, in the White House Situation Room, to view it firsthand. Now I'd like to know if you are coming."

"Fox, yes; NBC, yes; CBS, yes; ABC, yes."

"Thank you, I'll see you shortly."

"Mr. President, Dr. O'Brien is calling."

"Bill how is everything going, are you ready?"

"That's why I'm calling; I am."

"Good but we have to wait until 5:45; the news people won't be here until then. How does the situation look right now?"

"Mr. President I wish I could be upbeat, there are serious problems, but on a positive side of the things, some areas sustained received less damage than forecasted. However, we still don't know how the aftershocks will affect matters."

"Okay Bill, see you in an hour."

I need to sit down; the stress is unbelievable.

"Mr. President, everyone is here, including the Cabinet, and Admiral Timm."

"Thanks Mrs. Witt, now show them in."

"Congressman Peters it's good of you to come."

"Mr. President, this is Ray Oher Conoco/Phillips, Ted Stevenson ABC, David Mills NBC, Walter Smith CBS, and Christopher Dahl FOX."

"Folks, have a seat; I think you know the Cabinet, the Chief of Staff, Admiral Timm. The reason I asked you here was to give you a first-hand look at the situation in the Middle East. Let me warn you, it's very graphic. Now I'll turn things over to Dr. William O'Brien, Chairman of the Department of Geology and Earth Science at the University of Minnesota, Dr. O'Brien is a leading expert on subterranean earthquakes. It was Dr. O'Brien who first raised the possibility that a large earthquake would strike the Middle East and a smaller one in the Mississippi River Valley Basin. Dr. O'Brien, it's all yours."

"Thank you, Mr. President."

"Let me begin with some background information. There are three principal types or categories of faults, all can cause an earthquake: normal, reverse (or thrust) and strike slip. Reverse faults, like those along convergent plates, are ones associated most often with powerful quakes; those with a magnitude greater than 8. The quake that occurred in the

154

Middle East region had a magnitude greater than 9.5, and had a range of over 1,000 kilometers. Although we aren't completely sure, we think the depth of this quake was close to 500 kilometers, and had an effective destruction width of nearly 450 kilometers, though in some places, it could have been even higher. We also think the last time a quake of this magnitude, took place over 150,000 years ago. As such, our knowledge of such a massive quake is very limited. Now I'd like to show you a model that I helped put together, it will give you a better understanding of how massive this event was, plus a preview of the aftershocks to follow. I think the narrative will speak for itself."

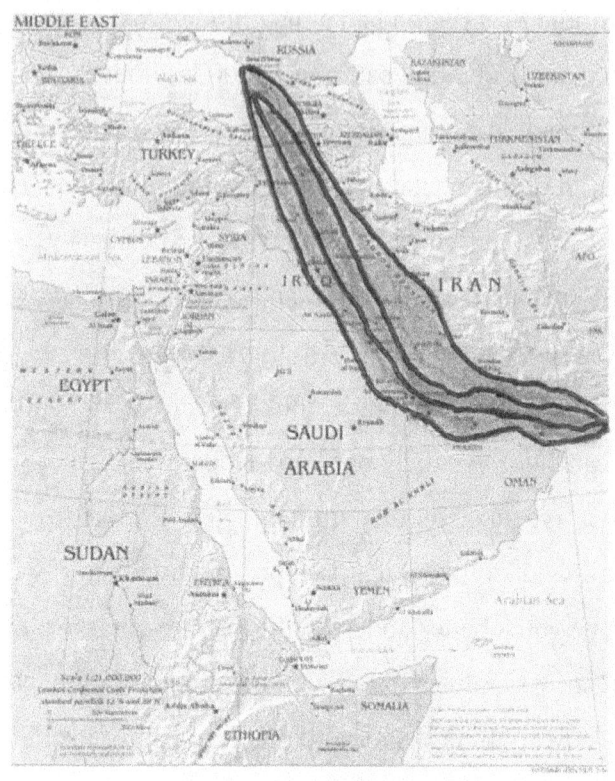

Primary & Secondary

Impact Zones

156

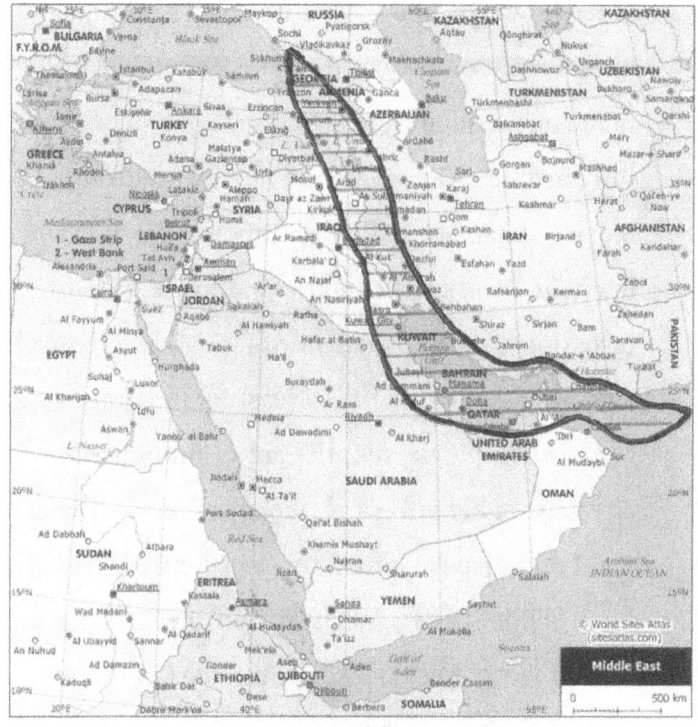

Impacted Cities

"Dr. O'Brien, Admiral Timm. I never imagined something this large could happen."

"Sir, it has; look at the satellite images from earlier today. Impressive aren't they."

"Mr. President." "Dr. O'Brien, thank you."

157

"Men, now you know what we're up against, as does the rest of the world. Many countries located in the quake zone were devastated, and may never fully recover. The amount of money needed to repair the damage will be enormous, at a time when many of those same countries are in the grips of recession. To make matters worse, Middle East oil supplies are now cut off, at least for the time being, God forbid if those supplies are compromised in any way, either now or by the aftershocks. Believe me, I don't have a holistic answer for this; I don't think anyone does. What we don't need, is a mass sell on Wall Street and see large sums of money leave the county or have widespread hoarding of oil and natural gas supplies. That's why I issued Executive Order 031618 this morning; we simply must have time to sort through this. People, if we don't do this now, I shudder to think of the consequences. It's time for us to come together and stop the political gamesmanship and infighting; this is no time for theatre. These are trying times, as President I want your personal assurances that we, and I do mean all of us, can work together towards solving these problems. I'm not going to kid you, it won't be easy and we'll likely disagree at times, but we must work through it. As leaders, we all have differing viewpoints; but we are Americans, and we can work together if we put our mind to it. So let's get this done, if not for yourself, do it for your family, do it for your country, do it because it's the right thing to do. What better legacy could you leave your children and grandchildren? Now that's all I have to say; thanks for coming; I'll be calling all of you very soon. Mr. Mills."

"Mr. President, speaking for myself, you have my full cooperation."

As I look around the room, I see most everyone is nodding their head yes. I also some teary eyes; maybe I struck a nerve.

This has been one hell of a day; it would be nice to forget all about it, at least for a little while. I

should call my old pal, Senator Olson, the junior
Senator from Minnesota and invite myself over.

"Mark, John Keller, would you mind if I come over to your place for a drink, I need to get away."

"Sure John."

"Great, I just have to arrange things with the Secret Service; I know they'll be happy about the short notice. I should be there around six thirty; maybe Betty could fix her fabulous meatballs."

"Hi, Mark. Betty."

"Mr. President, what took you so long?"
"I had to argue with the Secret Service; something about needing more time to secure the area; right now they have two square blocks roped off."

"How did you convince them?"

"I said I'm the President, and we're going. Betty, I think I smell something wonderful."

"You do Mr. President."

"John if you don't mind, Mr. President hasn't really sunk in yet, and guys I'd prefer if we don't talk politics tonight."

"That's fine by me Mr. President.

"Thanks Mark."

"By the way John, I have someone I'd like you to meet. President Keller, this is my cousin, Mary Louise Johnson."

"How do you do Miss Johnson."

I can't believe it, here is a beautiful, woman probably in her early forties, smiling at me and shaking my hand. I'm mesmerized; I think it could be a great night.

"Miss Johnson."

"Call me Mary."

"Mary what do you do for a living."

"I'm a professor of American literature at the University of Minnesota. Mr. President, do you mind if I ask you a personal question?"

"Not at all, although I might not answer it, nothing personal you understand."

"Where did you learn to sing like that?"

"Like what?"

"Sir, don't be coy with me, I heard you sing at President Leonard's funeral; you sang beautifully, though you missed pronounced a word."

"Only one, leave it to a professor to notice that; well you see I didn't have much time to practice."

"Mr. President, you have a wonderful smile?" "

I do." "Betty, is supper ready?"

"John, it's ready. Why don't you both have a seat?"

162

"Mark, Betty, thanks for a great meal, as always."
"John, do you have to leave so soon?"

"I'm afraid so, I have to fly down south in the morning to assess the damage caused by the earthquake and also confer with the governors."

"Mr. President, will I see you again?"

"I hope so Mary, how about a tour of the White House at some point."

"I'd love to, but I have to fly home on Sunday."

"Would Saturday work for you?"

"That sounds great."

"Mark, walk me out." "What's the story on her?"

"Is she married to her work?"

"What do you think of her?"

"I'm not sure; we'll see what happens."

Now for some rest, tomorrow will be a long day.

Day 7

Wednesday March 6 5:45am

"A fantastic meal and a good night's sleep sure works wonders. I hope the Director of the CIA and the Defense Secretary plan to join me today."

"Mr. Roberts, please call them just to be sure; and tell them Air Force One will lift off at 7:00."

"Mr. President, Marine 1 will pick you up at 6:30." "Is that okay?"

"Yes, that's fine." "Mrs. Witt."

"Mr. President, Admiral Timm is on the phone, he says it's urgent."

"Admiral, what can I do for you?"

"It seems the Russians are up to something in the Middle East."
"What exactly do you mean?"

164

"The latest satellite photos taken a little over an hour ago indicate a flotilla, consisting of four cruisers and five destroyers, is headed for the Gulf of Oman."

"Admiral if that's true, get together with the Joint Chiefs and prepare options. Also, send me a copy of those photos and all the latest reports we have on their movements; do it as soon as possible. If they aren't ready before I leave, have them transmitted to Air Force One (AF1)."

"I will sir, have a good flight."

"Mr. President, Marine One is standing by".

"Okay Wayne let's go."

"Good morning Mr. President, welcome aboard Marine One."

"Thanks Major, we can leave when you're ready." As we lift off, the sound of the whirring blades, reminds me of my first helicopter ride, on a Navy

HC-2. Then, we were lifting off the flight deck of the aircraft carrier John F. Kennedy; I was headed home, my tour was over. Now, as we are about to land at Andrews, I see two people waiting to greet me, the White House Press Secretary and an Air Force officer. I guess everyone else is already onboard, which is customary I assume. Upon boarding the plane, I notice a female Air Force officer standing next to the cockpit door; a male officer quickly joins her, both walk up to me.

"Mr. President, I'm John David, commander of Air Force One, this is Fran Murray my co-pilot."

"Mr. President, you probably don't remember me?"

"Colonel Murray you look familiar, but I can't place you."

"Sir, if I say graduate school, would that help you?"

"Let me think, I don't recall anyone named Fran, but I do remember a Francis, she was a student in my International Relations class."

"Mr. President, that was me, I'm Francis."

"Oh yes; the pretty one who never looked my way."

"Sir, I did to, you just didn't notice."

"Well Fran, it certainly is a small world, my first flight aboard Air Force One, and the co-pilot, a former classmate. Fran nice to see; we can talk later, but now we best get going."

As we taxi, I'm given a tour of the aircraft then took a seat; we're about to takeoff. Most people don't know the engines on AF1 have a thirty-five percent greater thrust than do conventional 747; thus, allow a faster climb in the case of an emergency.

"Wayne, have you talked to the governors today?"

"Sir, yes I have, they are meeting us at the Naval Air Station in Memphis."

I best review the latest reports and aerial photos of the affected areas before we arrive. Right after we land, I'm going to ask the governors to come aboard and to talk strategy.

"Wayne, when we leave, I want the Captain to fly over the quake zone(s) before heading home."

"Sir, I'll talk to him and get back to you."

As Wayne walks away, I'm handed a report which includes aerial photos of Russian movements within the Mediterranean. On the surface, it appears they're maneuvering to take control of the region, if they get a chance; not a good sign. Fortunately, it appears U.S. Carrier Group 7 is in a good position to block them. "Secretary Williams, let's talk."

"Have you looked at the data Admiral Timm sent?"

"Yes, I have and it's rather disturbing."

"What's your take on this?"

"Sir, I think we should move our carrier group closer in. If we do that, the Russians might rethink their position."

"Mr. Secretary, let's get Timm on the phone and talk this over."

"Sir, I'll call him now."

"Admiral, what do you make of Russian activity?"

"Mr. President, to them it might seem like a choice opportunity although I'm less certain of that."

"Should we move our carrier group back to their standard position, or move them closer in?"

"Sir, I think we should move then closer; it'll let the Russians know, we aren't going away."

"Admiral, I think State and I should talk to the Russian Ambassador. Wayne, get in touch with the Secretary of State, have her arrange a meeting with the Ambassador for tomorrow. Admiral, thanks for your help, I'll call you again when I get back."

"Mr. President." "Yes what is it Martin?"

"A reporter would like to ask you a few questions."

"Martin, I don't know if I should do that, I don't have time to take questions, and if I talked to her, that won't be fair to the others (i.e. reporters)."

"Could you at least come by and say hi, she has bugged me ever since we left?"

"Okay I'll say hello, but that's all."

Now that's over, I need to get up and move.

As I return to my seat, I hear Colonel Murray calling me.

"Mr. President, do you have a moment?"

"Yes, Colonel what is?"

"Sir, I should warn you, there's a severe thunderstorm approaching; we may have to circle and wait until it passes."

"Colonel you and the Captain are in charge, do what you need to do. Is there anything else?"

There is one thing, and I might be getting ahead of myself, but I want to ask you anyway."

"Go ahead ask."

"Colonel David is retiring next month, and I'd like take his place, if that's alright with you."

"Certainly, if you're qualified, I see no problem."

"Sir, we were once classmates and now both widowed. Will that cause a problem?"

"Not in the least." Then briefly I see a look that troubles me.

What am I missing? Does she have her eye on me? She's quite attractive but I don't want to date.

So why am I attracting women as of late; is it me or is it the Presidency? I think it's the later. Still, in the six days since taking office, I've witnessed overtones from several women; only one knew me before hand. You know, I shouldn't be wasting my time thinking about this? I have more important matters to attend to; I need to get back to work.

Upon fastening my seat belt, the plane begins its descend; the thunderstorm has passed us by. Upon landing, taxi to a secured area near the far end of the field. There the governors and I will review photos and study reports from the quake sites.

Looking out the right side of the plane, I see the governors coming into view. Governor Murray, Governor Petersen, Governor Edwards, Governor Jensen; they're all here. I wish it were under better circumstances.

"Mr. President, on behalf of all of us, thanks for coming; we have a lot to go over; so, we decided to set it up in the hanger." "Is that okay with you?"

"Sure, of course."

"Len how's the family? It's been far too long."

"They're fine; come and visit when you can."

"Tom, Jerry, Joe, how are you guys?"

"Sir, good all things considered."

The last time I saw these boys was at the governor's conference, and we had a blast. Nine months later, look where we are, in Memphis, in a hangar handling a crisis.

"Sir, you have far more troubling problems have."

"That might be true, but Len, yours are no less important. Looks like everything is ready, should we sit down?"

"Mr. President, this is Mike Burrows, our regional civil defense director; he's going to walk us through the photos and site maps, and then review death and injury reports. Mike."

"Mr. President, as you can see from the map the earthquake started here, approximately five miles south southwest of Saratoga Kentucky. From there, the quake headed south along the Mississippi River, entering Missouri approximately ten miles west of the river; then headed south to a point just east of Blytheville Arkansas. From that position, it moved south southeast back over the river into Tennessee, on a line some four to five miles east of the river, ending at a point approximately ten miles due west of Covington, Tennessee. The latest data indicates seismic activity ranged from 6.2 to 7.1 on the Richter."

"We know, sporadic structural and infrastructure damage occurred in a few urban areas, but the majority of damage took place in farm country.

174

Widespread flooding and dead livestock, the biggest concern. Fortunately, there were no deaths reported, at least so far; injuries we estimate at about four hundred, but we 're awaiting positive confirmation; the reports we have now, list injuries that range from bumps and bruises, to fractures, to head/ back trauma."

"Final damage estimates have not been complied, but we believe private property damage could be in the neighborhood of fifty to seventy million, public property closer to a hundred. Yet, it could've been worse. I think early preparation was the key. We had rescue and medical personnel on site, as soon as conditions allowed. Also there was plenty of food and supplies."

"Mr. Burrows I think much of the credit goes to the governors; they knew what needed to be done, and did it. Fellows, at this point, what else do you need from the Federal Government? I have FEMA standing by; I asked the Army Corp of Engineers to help with infrastructure."

"Mr. President, speaking for myself and I'm sure the other governors would concur, you've been extremely helpful; being a governor yourself you know how difficult disasters can be."

"Len thanks for those kind words, I sure do appreciate it. Now I'd like to fly over the area if you don't mind. Does anyone want to ride along; supper at the White House is on me."

"Sir, I think we should get back."

"I should to, I have a mess waiting for me."

As AF1 pulls away from the hangar, I couldn't help but think how a President and four southern governors were able to work together and get things done, without politics getting in the way. I'm sure it helped that we were well acquainted, and that I was once in their shoes. As AF1 leveled off, I was finally able to relax. As we neared the quake zone, Colonel David reported that a large cloudbank had recently formed over the area; the ceiling, less than 2,500 feet. For security reason, AF1 is not allowed to cruise under below 4,000; therefore, we won't be able to view the area.

Anticipation turned to disappointment. As we ascended to cruising altitude; I get a call from Amanda Jensen, the assistant Press Secretary, and my assistant.

"Hi Amanda, glad your back. How is your dad?"

"He's much better now. Mr. President, the Treasury Secretary just called me, and he says he wants to see you right away, he said it's urgent."

"Tell him to meet me in the White House at 3:00; and tell him to bring the Energy Secretary along and if possible, the Chairman of Stock Exchange. We'll be landing at Andrews shortly after 2:00. What else do you have?"

"Sir, it can wait."

"If it's important, give it to me now."

"The Secretary of State told me the Russian ambassador may not wish to meet with you."

"Alright, I deal with that when I get back."

The Russians can never give a firm commitment on anything. Now I need to outline my financial and energy plan in preparation for the meeting. I wish I could say it is nice to be back; it seems I never left.

"Mrs. Witt, get Ambassador Dobrenin on the phone." I've heard he's a character; oh well, he can't be any worse than some of our legislators.

"Ambassador Dobrenin, President Keller, how are you sir?"

"Fine, Mr. President."

"That's good, the reason I'm calling is about tomorrow's meeting. It's good that can meet and hash out some. I know you're busy, so am I; but think a get together is important. Can I count on speaking with you tomorrow?"

"Alright, Mr. President, if you insist."

"Okay, see you at 10:30, good day sir."

Nothing like pulling teeth, maybe he wanted to jockey me around; good luck with that.

"Mr. President, the Treasury and Energy Secretaries are here; I'm told the Exchange Chairman should be along in a few minutes." "Show them in Mrs. Witt."

"Ron, Jim, come in, have a seat. Have you folks given any thought to what we talked about?"

"Sir, yes we have but we also have some questions." "I have some to." "Come in Mr. Emery, this is Jim Wilson, our Energy Secretary, you already know Mr. Coles. Shall we get right to it?"

Here it is; we now have four days to outline a plan for handling this crisis. I know big oil and the Wall Streeter(s) would like to strangle me, but I had to do something, and fast. Trust me, if I didn't, we'd have had a major crisis to deal with; not good. So where does that leave us."

"If we were energy independent, which we aren't, it would be no big deal. But we aren't, that's why we need a plan to stabilize things, and thus position ourselves for the long term; void of Middle East oil. Jim, where are we sitting now?"

"Mr. President, currently fifteen percent of our oil needs comes from the Persian Gulf, mainly light crude. Another twenty-five percent from Canada, and for now that looks secure, but you never know. The remainder comes from domestic sources. Thankful we don't have to import natural gas."

"So, fellows, how can we fill a fifteen percent void? One suggestion I'm hearing, we mandate cars and trucks run on natural gas, which the big three and the Japanese automakers tell me it can be done. They also tell me they can inexpensively convert nearly all vehicles produced over the last two years. The biggest hang-up, constructing natural gas fueling stations; to date big oil has blocked nearly every attempt to do that. It's critical that we get their support to make this happen. So, Secretary Wilson, if we can get everyone on board how soon will we see changes implemented sufficient enough to make a substantial difference?"

"Sir, my best guess is eighteen months, perhaps longer. Wilson, that's too long; we need to have everything in place sooner than that. What we need is a declaration of war; a war on usage."

"So fellows, what will happen to the price of crude oil in the meantime? $100 a barrel, $200 a barrel; does anyone really know. That's why we need Wall

Street and big oil, hell we need everyone onboard. Our economic well-being is at stake. All must bring something to the table; and all must bear the pain."

"Mr. Emery you've been quiet, what do you think?"

"Mr. President, I think your plan might work." "Do you have anything else?"

"Sir, we'll hear lots of bitching and complaining, and I think we all knew that. Still, if we move forward, and it fails, your political future is over."

"Mr. Emery, the only future I have in mind is one where my children, my grandchildren and everyone else in this country will live in peace and in relative comfort. If people want to throw me under the bus, so be it; but now it's time to act, end the talk, and start the walk."

"Here's what I want you men to do; I want you to put your ideas on paper, do it now. On Thursday afternoon, I'll invite all the players: Wall Street, Big

Oil, the Carmakers, Congressional Leaders, the Chamber of Commerce, leading academics, and a handful of citizens to the White House for an in-depth briefing. People, this is big, bigger than all of us; time to get united. Now that's all I have to say."

"Sir, we're on it".

"Mr. President, you have a call."

"Who is it Mrs. Witt?"

"It's your sister-in-law."

"Hi, Lynn how can I help?"

"I'm back in town."

"I didn't know you we were planning to return. If the trip was necessary, why didn't you call ahead?"

"John, I needed to talk to you in person."

"Well, come on over; by the way where are you, should I send a car?"

"I'm at the airport, please do send a car."

"Okay, stay put until Colonel Shaw arrives."

"Mrs. Witt, go down the hall and have Colonel Shaw come to my office, immediately."

"Colonel, I want you to take an unmarked car and go pick up my sister-in-law at the airport and bring her here, use the rear entrance. I'll explain later."

"Lynn, come in, Colonel if you don't mind. Please sit down, relax. Now what's wrong?"

"John, ever since I got back home, I had a feeling someone was following me. Also, in the past few days I've received a host of weird text messages, all from unknown numbers."

"Did you respond?" "No, I just deleted them all."

"Lynn, let me make a call."

"Mr. Attorney General, has the Secret Service completed that assignment I gave you?"

"Yes sir."

"Good, thanks."

"Mrs. Witt, check and see if the FBI Director is still in the building, he was here for a briefing."

"John, what's going on?"

"That's what I want to find out. Maybe it has something to do with what you found the other day. If the President's death is the result of foul play, I'm sure the people involved don't want it known."

"Mr. President the Director is on his way up."
"Lynn I'm sorry I got you into this mess I don't want to see you get hurt."

"John, I know."

"Come in director; Lynn this is FBI Director Lloyd Bonds. Please, both of you have a seat. Mr. Bonds, what I'm about to tell you stays in this room, are we clear about that?"

"Perfectly clear Mr. President."

"Lynn besides being my sister-in-law she is an excellent internist and pathologist. I asked Lynn to join the autopsy team to assist in the examination President Leonard's body. What she found, but never revealed to anyone else, except me, was the presence of mutated bacteria in the President's bloodstream. This type of bacteria just recently discovered, and initially thought to be harmless, at least that's what the scientists tell me. Later it was discovered should the bacteria mutate it could prove fatal for someone having certain health condition(s). That's what we think happened in the President's case. Since returning home, Lynn felt she was being followed, in addition to receiving weird text messages at all hours."

"Director, I want you to look into this matter; also, I want an agent assigned to her. I think it best if she returns home tonight, so not to raise any suspicion."

"Mr. President, you know that'll take some time."

"I understand Director; Lynn will stay here and make flight arrangements; call us when you have the agent assigned and he/she is ready to travel."

"Yes sir."

"Mr. Bonds I want your agent to be on the plane with her but refrain from questioning her."

"Mr. President, this is a serious."

"Director, it is, but now I need to focus my attention on other matters; we've done all we can, for now."

"I understand Mr. President; I'll keep you inform."

"Lynn, would you like anything special for dinner?"

"Oh, something light, I'm not very hungry."
"I'll have what you're having, but right now I'm going to have a drink, care to join me?"

"John, maybe I shouldn't say this, but something seems to be drawing us together, but why and for what reason, I haven't a clue."

"I hear you, but with all the things going, I can't make sense of it either, I just have to put it aside, at least for now.

The next few hours could be the only time I have to relax and unwind; and I plan to take advantage of it." Then she's gone.

Day 8

Thursday March 7 5:45am

"Mr. President, good morning."

"Good morning Amanda (Amanda Jensen, Assistant Press Secretary); please come in."

"Who's that Harvard professor you keep talking about?"

"Do you mean Milton Lewis?"

"Yes, that's him. He's that Russian expert."

"He is, but not everyone thinks so, his opinions are a bit off the wall."

"Can he be trusted; and keep his mouth shut?"

"I think so but why do you ask?"

"I need someone outside the diplomatic circle who will give me an unbiased opinion about our Soviet 'friends'. Would you mind calling him, and invite him here for a meeting?"

"Not at all, when?"

"Today; but maybe that's out of the question since he lives in Cambridge."

"No, it's not he's in town today for a book signing."
"Well call him; see when he's available."

"Mr. President, he can be here at 1:30."

"Let me check my calendar. Mrs. Witt, what do I have scheduled for this afternoon?"

"Sir, you have a meeting with Congressional leaders at 3:00, and a noon luncheon with the Treasury

Secretary." "Thanks." "Amanda, have him be here at 1:30."

"Sir, do you want me here?"

"Yes, for the introductions, State and I'll talk to him alone."

"Sir, I understand."

"Amanda, I have reports to review before the ambassador gets here, so if you'll excuse me."

"Mrs. Witt, let me know when Secretary Conrad arrives."

"She has."

"Vickie (a.k.a. Vickie Conrad, newly appointed Assistant Secretary of State, formerly with Commerce) please have a seat, how is your day?"

"Okay."

"Vickie the ambassador won't be here for at least an hour, so let's talk strategy before he arrives."

"Mr. President, before we get into that, let me update you on a couple of things. As of this morning, our allies decided to support the position as presented in your Executive Order; but that could change if things turn chaotic. Also, as of now, we're remain on friendly terms with Russia and China, and most of the Middle Eastern with a couple of exceptions; primarily Iran and Syria. On the down-side, several Muslim clerics suggest the United States somehow caused the quake, how crazy is that; crazier still, some are starting to believe the claim. I guess they feel a need to blame someone, why not us."

"You know, I expected as much; but now on to the subject at hand."

"Sir, when I spoke to the Russian Foreign Minister about Naval movements, he denied there was anything out of the ordinary; just routine operations.

When I showed him satellite images taken yesterday, he got very defensive, and said "America is sticking its nose in places where it doesn't belong." Then he politely excuses himself, saying he's late for a meeting, then I came here."

"What's your take?" "Do we play hardball?"

"Sir, I think we must remind the Russians as to our longstanding interest in the Middle East, that of protecting America's oil interest and insuring safety of our allies. Our position hasn't changed; it remains the same despite the devastating quake. That's what I think we should tell the Ambassador when he arrives."

"Vickie, I agree; after our meeting with Dobrenin, I want you to prepare a letter for the Russian President, wherein you reaffirm our position. I'll sign it when it's ready."

"I can do that."

"Mrs. Witt." "Sir, the Russian Ambassador is here." "Show him in."

"Mr. Ambassador, please come in, you know Secretary Conrad."

"Thank you Mr. President, madam Secretary. Mr. President, please accept our condolences on the untimely death of President Leonard. My country looks forward to working with you and your administration."

"Ambassador Dobrenin, thank you. Sir, the reason I asked you here is that I wish to discuss the Middle East. The tragic events of the last few days have changed the dynamics of the area and the world, particularly when it comes to oil and its financial impact on world markets. In response to that, we have begun the process of defining the measures we need to take, given the circumstances, short and long term. I'd expect Russia and other countries will do the same.

"I think it's absolutely essential that we keep the lines of communication open, but especially during this difficult period. Events brought about from a natural disaster, in my view, shouldn't escalate tensions between us. Secretary Conrad, as you may know, has already talked to your Foreign Minister about specific naval movements. Ambassador, our position on the Middle East and the entire Mediterranean has not changed. We are there to protect our interests and help maintain the safety of our allies. What is Russia's position?"

"Mr. President, Russia's position hasn't changed either; moving naval forces, as always, ongoing, as is yours. We're a peaceful country; we only wish to see the region stable."

"Mr. Ambassador I'd like to believe that. Yet it seems inevitable that our counties will disagree. As such, I'd like you to setup a meeting with President Illioff, so that we can discuss such matters more fully. What do you think, can you do that?"

"Mr. President, I'll send your request along."

"Thank you Mr. Ambassador, the Secretary will walk you out. Vickie, I'll see you later."

As the ambassador walks away, I hear him say **"Что ошибочной дурак этом"** in English; it translates as "what a misguided fool he is."

Well it's nice to know what he thinks of me personally, what he doesn't know, I understand what he said, I just don't speak the language. For now, that's my secret; only few know I understand the language, thankfully no one in government.

Well that was an interesting lunch; the Treasury Secretary is something else; all he wants to talk about is how much money Wall Street could lose. He's right, but only to a point, they will lose some, but they'll survive, we're just asking them to hold the line. One of my commanding officers once said, "Officers must look after the little guy; the big guys will take care of themselves". That's the truth?

"Mr. President, Professor Jewison is here." "Thank you Mrs. Witt, show him in."

"Professor Jewison, John Keller, please have a seat. Sir, Amanda speaks highly of you; she suggested I talk with you and listen to what you have to say."

"Mr. President, you didn't invite me here just to shoot the breeze." "Quite right, I did not; Amanda told me you would speak your mind. So, I'll get straight to the point; tell me everything you know about Russia, present tense. From your perspective, what are they up to?"

"Sir, how much time do you have?"

"I have ninety minutes."

"Well we better get started."

"Over the last six months, the militant faction of the Communist Party has been gaining strength and has successfully gotten more of its people into positions of authority. These militants are what we used to call hard liners. They believe Russia should a major player in the world, regardless of the risk."

"Professor, aren't they concerned about China?"

"It's interesting that you bring that up; the hard liners think China is fractionalized and gotten too capitalistic to be a threat, should Russia choose to pursue a course of world domination."

"How close are the militants from taking control?"

"My guess and it's just a guess, maybe five years, perhaps longer, so there is time. You know Russia never speaks with one voice, but two conflicting ones. Those polarizing views are the military and the diplomatic corps; one rarely talks to other and both go out of their way to undercut the other. This makes for a volatile situation."

"Professor Jewison, where does President Illioff stand in all of this?"

"Unfortunately, he seems to favor the military, but only for political reasons. I think, in his heart, he knows where it might end up; still he'd like us to think, war is unthinkable."

"Well Professor Jewison, I enjoyed talking to you. If you don't mind, I'd like to keep in touch. Perhaps we meet again and talk some more."

"Mr. President I'd be more than happy to."

"I just finished a brief on the latest power struggle in that country; I can send you a copy if you like."

"Yes, please do."

"Martin what's all the excitement?"

"Sir, please turn on your TV and switch to the Fox-News Channel. Their senior correspondent for financial matters is about to vilify you on your decision to suspend trading on Wall Street; he's about to speak."

"On Tuesday, President Keller issued an Executive Order that suspends Wall Street trading for five days, maybe more. We're incensed by this action; furthermore, we believe he lacks the legal authority to do so. We call upon him to lift the suspension, and do it immediately. We also condemn the President for freezing the price of oil and natural gas. It's our belief the earthquake in the Middle East will have no effect on financial markets."

"Who is this birdbrain, who put him up to this?"

"Sir, the information we hear, it was the Chairman of the Stock Exchange, and the Chair of BP."

"Get the President of Fox News and the Chairman of the Exchange on the phone; do it now. It seems the only thing these guys care about is lining their pockets; they don't give a dam about the country, only themselves."

"Mr. Dahl, Mr. Emery, President Keller, men, I just finished watching a disturbing piece on Fox.

Would you care to explain yourselves? Don't you people care about this country, and its future?"

"Mr. President, this is Mr. Emery. Sir, we don't think it was the right decision."

"Tell me you so called experts what would you have me do; nothing I suspect. Fellows, let me tell you what would have happen if I listened to you."

"First, the price of oil and gasoline would have tripled or quadrupled almost immediately. Second, there would've been a massive sell off on Wall Street, with most stocks nose diving; resulting in businesses, individuals, and families experiencing heavy losses. Third, hoarding of oil and gas supplies would have begun almost immediately. The only people to profit from all of this activity would be the oil tycoons and Wall Street traders. You people seem to care more about yourselves than you do about the homeland. We need time to develop a plan of action, while maintaining the status quo; right now we're in the process of putting that plan together as we speak. Instead of waiting to see what we come up with, each of you decided to stir things up. What you have succeeded in doing is making an already difficult situation worse. Our people need assurances, all you've given them is uncertainty and doubt."

"Sir, on behalf of Fox News I apologized."
"That's fine Mr. Dahl, but I need something more than that from you. I need you to tell your viewers that there was a rush to judgment; therefore the President should be allowed sufficient time to put his plan in place; a plan that will benefit all Americans. Will you do that Mr. Dahl?"
"Yes Mr. President, I'll see to it personally."

"Mr. Emery, what do you have to say?"

"Sir, I to apologize, Wall Street will work with you on this."

"Fellows, if we do this right, everyone will benefit; new opportunities will present themselves, but it will take time. Now if you'll excuse me, I've a meeting with Congressional leaders."

"Martin, do think I was too hard on them?" "No Mr. President, they deserved it, especially Emery; you would expect it from Fox but not from the Chairman of the Stock Exchange."

"Martin, I'm not going to let them or Congress, push me around and cause more delays. The days of feet dragging are over; now see if the Congressional leaders are here."

"Come in people; we have some work to do. Amanda please bring in the workbooks and setup the screen, I'm going to use it for my Power-Point. Before we begin, I want to remind you and other members of Congress, we're in this together; this is not about Democrats, Republicans or Independents, this is about setting a new course for America, given the events that have occurred in the Middle East, relative to oil supplies. We don't need anyone to speak out-of-hand, just to score political points. If someone chooses that course, they'll be held accountable. I know this is hard on everyone, I don't like it any better than you do, but dam-it we're stuck with it, and it's up to us, as leaders, to fix it. The past week tested our resolve; so far we have held our own."

"In your workbook, you'll find several workable suggestions/solutions that need consideration and approval, to solve immediate issues and to set a course for the long haul; all essential to make the concept work. Can I guarantee success; no, I can't; I don't think anyone can. This is uncharted territory; the future, unknown. Like I said before, time is of the essence. Now any questions before I begin? Miss Jensen the lights if you please."

That went well, I think.

"Thank you for your attention, remember I need concurrence on every item listed in Section 1, and I need it by noon tomorrow. If I have it by then, I will let trading resume; Wall Street can open for business starting next Tuesday; if not, the suspension will continue until approval is received. Know the petroleum and automobile industries have conditions they must approve. Have a good day."

"Wayne, how do you think it went?"

Sir, you spelled it out well, clear and precise."

"Do you think they got the message, or can we expect more of the same?"

"I certainly hope they did, time will tell. So Wayne, how about a drink, I think we can use one"

Darn, I almost forgot, I have to call the children and let them know about Sunday. I hope to fly home and spend the day with them; I need to get away from this place. "Amanda, ask the Air Force and Secret Service to prepare for a Sunday trip to Minnesota." Now for a short walk. While standing outside, I see a flock of birds fly over the White

House, and in the distance, I see a group of people about to enter the South Lawn, about twenty yards to the left of me. Now that's bit odd, so late in the afternoon; it's nearly six o'clock. So I ask my Secret Service agent to go over and investigate. As it turns out, it's a business education group from Minnesota; they were given permission to visit the grounds since they were denied access to the White House this late in the day. Given these are home folks; I should walk over and say hi. They certainly aren't expecting me. After a few handshakes, it's time to leave, then, I hear a familiar voice.
"Mr. President". "Well Professor Johnson, it's nice to see you again."

"It's nice to see you sir, and please call me Mary."

"All right Mary."

"So, what are you doing here?"

"John, the symposium we were attending at the Department of Commerce ran late; it was scheduled to end at 3:30; after that we were slated for a quick tour of the White House, but the four o'clock deadline has passed; so instead we were given the option of touring the grounds."

"Mary, what are you doing later?" "I'm going back to the hotel, have supper and read."

"Professor, would you like to have dinner at the White House, as my guest?" "Are you serious, of course I would?" "Unfortunately, Mary I can't invite your friends."

"Sir, we don't have to tell them; I'll say I made other arrangements for the night."

"When the tour is finished, stop by the front gate, I'll have a pass waiting for you; a Secret Service agent will escort you in. I'm going to ask the White House chef to schedule dinner for seven thirty." "Is that alright?"

"That's perfect."

"Good, see you then."

"Mary it's nice of you to come. Is this your first visit to the White House?"

"Yes sir, it is."

"Well then, let me show you around, we have some time before dinner. Are there any rooms you want to see?"

"I'd like to see the East Room and the Oval Office if it's not too much trouble."
"It's no trouble, anything else?"

"If we have time, maybe the Lincoln bedroom, I hear it's beautiful."

I then decide to turn around and look directly at her; I could see her cheeks were red, her eyes sparkling. When I was younger, I might have interpreted her posture differently. Still for the longest time, I didn't know what to say, except to say "oh, if you wish"; then change the subject.

During dinner, she does most of the talking; I remain an attentive listener. Then suddenly and very unexpectedly, she says, "Are you seeing anyone?"

"Mary, I'm a little busy these days."

I thought that would end it, but she appears unmoved.

"Why would any man who is President of the United States, handsome and single and has a beautiful voice have trouble attracting women."

"Thanks for the compliment. Maybe when I return to private life, I'll have more time to socialize."

"Mark tells me your wife died in an automobile accident."

"Yes, she was killed by a drunk driver, four years ago this July."

"I miss her a lot; fortunately, I have my children and grandchildren; but enough about me. Why hasn't an attractive woman like you found someone to settle down with?"

"Either I'm unlucky or picky, maybe some of both."

At this point, I decided to bring the evening to a close before things get out of hand. As much as I'm attracted to her and her to me, I'm certainly not in a position to take it further. I have a job to do, and it's an important one. The media would love a story; I'm not going to give them one.

"Mary I'd like to thank you for a wonderful evening, I enjoyed our time together. Unfortunately, I have some reading to do before I retire; the Secret Service will drive you back."

"Thank you so much Mr. President, can I give you a hug before I leave."

"Sure."

That came as no surprise, what came next did.

As I stepped back, she gently grabs the back of my neck and pulls me forward and gives me a passionate kiss on the lips. I felt as if I was in a dream; the last time I had a kiss like that, I was with my wife. To hide my obvious pleasure, I quickly walked to the door and summon the Secret Service.

"Agent, please take Professor Johnson to her hotel."

To say the least, I was shocked and confused. I don't know what to make of it; best to forget and concentrated on more important matters; I know that's easier said than done. She is fine looking woman, there is no denying that.

Day 9

Friday, March 8 5:15 am

Time to get up; has it been only four hours, I kept waking up thinking about last evening. It must be the office; it seems more than a few people who had this job had challenges that involved women. I do enjoy the attention; best not to cross the line. Well enough of that nonsense; time to read the morning paper for a little 'uplifting' inspiration, not. Well that's interesting; the Times states, "The reason we took military action in the Persian Gulf was to counter Russian naval activity, after the earthquake.

"Wayne, good morning, put a call into Cromwell at the Times; I need to talk to him about his story in the morning edition. Amanda, call Admiral Timm, tell him I need to see him right away."

Andy Leonard may have let his people leak stories; but I won't. In my view, if I tell someone that information is confidential it is to remain confidential; not for distribution. My rule, one and you're done; you're gone.

"Mr. Cromwell, President Keller. I want to talk about your story in the morning Times. Don't give me that crap about an informed source; just tell me who gave you that information. No, I'm not going to comment, except to say the region will remain volatile for some time. Our job is to look after American interests and help our allies, if asked. Do you know about my policy regarding leaks? You may like to remind your informants before they open their mouth; having said that I still want a good working relationship with the press, but not if it effects security. As always, I will respond to all queries in a timely manner. If you wish to speak to me directly, just call my Press Secretary, he can arrange it. Thank you for your time, good day."

"Admiral, come in; have you read the morning Times, specifically Cromwell's story?"
"No I haven't." "Take a few minutes to read it."

"I want to know who leaked the info to Cromwell; when I talked to him, he said it came from Defense. I want you to track it down and get back to me. President Leonard may have been lax, but I'm not. One leak, you're gone. We can't afford to have our plans compromised, simply because someone needs to talk. While you're at it, please have the defense team assemble for a meeting; I want a reassessment of our operational strategy."

"Mr. President, I'll take care of it."

"Fine, let's shoot for 10:00 in the Situation Room; see you then. Mrs. Witt, have the Press Secretary meet me in the Oval Office as soon as he can."

"Martin, come in, have a seat. Have you read the morning Times? What do you think about the Cromwell story? I asked Admiral Timm to investigate the source of the leak; Cromwell said it came from defense. My policy on leaks is strict, one you're done. I can't afford people who can't keep quiet. No one is exempt. Do you have any questions?" "No."

"Okay enough of that, now let's talk about my address tomorrow night."

"If Congress, big oil, and the auto industry approve my plan by noon tomorrow, I plan to go before the

American people and explain our strategy. I'll also announce the resumption of trading and rescind the band on capital transfers. However, the freeze on exports of gasoline and related products will remain in place until we know the industry is stable. I want you and your staff to help with my presentation. Given the complexity and time constraints, we need to start right now. Are we clear?"

"Yes sir." "Good, now make the necessary arrangements and assemble your team."

"Mr. President"

 "Mrs. Witt" "Sir your daughter is on the phone."

"Honey, what's wrong?"

"Dad about ten minutes ago a man came to my door; and identified himself as a Secret Service agent. When I asked to see some identification, he got mad. He said he had to search the house for security reasons."

"Elizabeth, was anyone with him?" "No, he appeared to be alone; at least I didn't see anyone." "What did you do?" "I told him he had to leave, now wasn't a good time."

"Did he go?"

"Sort of, he headed to his car, he's now standing next to it."

"Honey stay on the phone; I'm going to call the head of the Secret Service; I'll put you on speaker so I can still hear you while I'm talking to the him. Stay calm; we'll get to the bottom of this." "Okay Dad, please hurry, Susie will be waking up soon."

"Director Ericson, President Keller, my daughter just called me and said one of your Secret Service agents is at her door, wanting to come in and inspect the home; he's alone."

"Do you have an agent there, and if so what's he up to?" I still have her on the line."

"Mr. President, I have to make a few calls, do you want to stay on the line?"

"Yes, I do; Elizabeth he's checking on it now."

"Dad, the fellow looks like he's getting ready to leave. What should I do?"

"Honey, your cell phone has a camera doesn't it?"

"Yes, it does."

"Well take a picture of him, and if he starts to drive away, take a shot of his license plate."

"Okay Dad, I'm doing it now."

"Mr. President, that fellow isn't one of ours."

"Director, where are your agents, they're suppose to be protecting my family?"

"Mr. President, I don't know, I'll check into it."

"Ericson, I want this fellow apprehended and get your agents there pronto. Do you understand?"

"Yes."

"Fine, I'll expect a call when your men are in place and that fellow is in custody. After that, I want you to tell me why there was a breach in security."

"Elizabeth, stay on the phone until the Secret Service arrives; I still have you on speaker."
Now I'm going to call David and fill him in on what's happening.

"David, has a Secret Service agent been on duty since you returned home?"

"No, pop, I haven't seen one."

"I was afraid of that; we're in the process of fixing that. Please call me when they introduce themselves, and don't forget to ask for credentials."

"Director Ericson, I just spoke to my son and he said no one from the Secret Service was on duty when he arrived home. Therefore, I want a full report of this incident, by this evening; and I want you to deliver your report in person."

"Dad, the local police just arrived and took the fellow into custody. The Police Chief is coming up the walk."

"Honey, tell the Chief I'd like to talk to him."

"Dad, here he is."

"Chief, President Keller, how are you sir?"

"Good Mr. President."

"Chief, I like you to assign a police officer to stay with my daughter until the Secret Service arrives. I will personally cover the cost to your department."

"Sir, we'll be happy to."

"Great, I appreciate your help; can I speak to my daughter."

"Honey, everything is taken care of, I'm going to hang up now. Love you, please hug the kids."

Now where was I.

"Admiral Timm, come in."

"Mr. President the Joint Chiefs and the Defense Secretary are here; they're all waiting in the Situation Room."

Well that meeting was certainly a waste of time. Two and a half hours of military double talk; bottom line, nothing has changed. They could've said that in ten minutes. I suppose it comes down to job security. I always thought we were top heavy in the upper ranks, now I know it.

After all that, I now have just twenty minutes to speak with Senator Roth and the House Speaker concerning pending legislation.

"Mr. President, I have the Senator and the Speaker on the line."

"Senator, Mr. Speaker, thanks for taking my call. My time is brief, as is yours, so I'll get right to the point. Where do we stand; do we have the votes?'

"Mr. President, House members are still grumbling, some loudly." "Well what are they saying?" "They want to know why you doing this now; they think things will work out on their own; and besides, what will they get in return, those kinds of things."

"Mr. Speaker, we need support from both sides of the isle. I can understand their feelings, but we simply can't sit back and do nothing, there's too much at stake."

"Mr. President, I agree; I think we can muster 270 votes, possibly 300." "Thank you Speaker."

"Senator, how do things look in the Senate?" "Sir, right now, we have fifty-three, possibly fifty-seven votes." "Is the support balanced?" "No it's not; the Republicans are dragging their feet."

"Is it the issues, or are they just opposed to anything the President sends their way."

"Sir, I think it's a little of both." "Can you bring them around?"

"Sir, if we're lucky perhaps six maybe seven." "Fellows we need a two-thirds majority in each chamber. If you need anything, call me immediately. I'm planning on speaking to the nation tomorrow evening and lay out my plan and announce the resumption of trading and capital transfers. What time is the vote scheduled?"

"The House votes at 10:30; the Senate 11:45." "I'll call you both prior to the roll call."

"Mrs. Witt, I'm going to the Situation Room, send the Joint Chiefs, the Defense Secretary and Mr. Roberts there when they arrive." Given Russian naval maneuvers, I wonder what the brass has for me, it should be interesting.

"Fellows come in, let's get started I have a lot going on today. Admiral Timm, I think we should hear from the Navy first."

"Sir, I agree; Admiral Henry, take us back a few days, to when you first observed the Russian maneuvers." "Thank you Admiral Timm, Mr. President, on Monday, at approximately six AM our time; the Russian Navy had three heavy cruisers and a destroyer operating in the Ionian Sea, approximately 75 miles south southeast of the Gulf of Taranto; two other destroyers were located approximately 100 miles due west. Since that time, they've sailed east and are now located along the southern coast of Oman. Yesterday afternoon, around 4:00, we observed two Russian submarines and three light cruisers departing the south end of the Bay of Bengal; they're now located here about 150 miles south southwest of Bombay and appear to be on a westerly course. We suspect the movements are not routine exercises. Admiral, show me where the Six Fleet is now. Sir, the Harry

S. Truman along with three destroyers, a supply ship and a tanker, are here, some sixty miles off the coast of Syria."

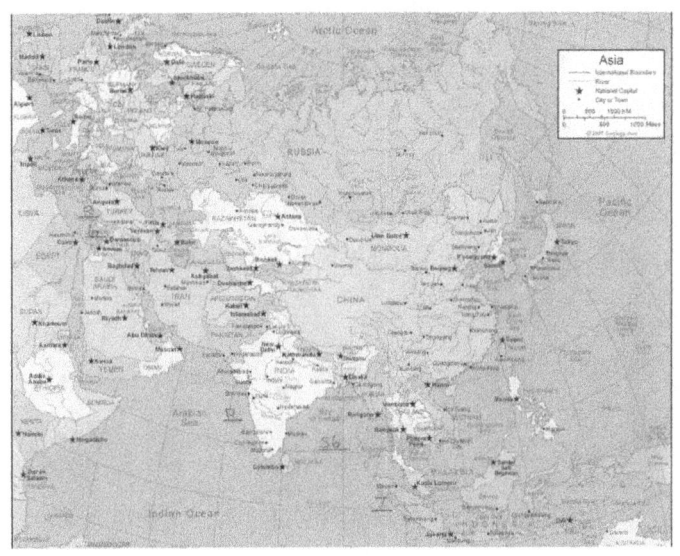

Russian and U.S. Naval Positions
R= Russian Flotilla, 6=US 6th Fleet, 7=US 7th Fleet, S6=US Submarine Task Force 6

"Do we have any ships operating in the Indian Ocean?" "Sir, we have Submarine Task Force Six operating along the southern end of the Bay of Bengal." "How many submarines are in Task Force

Six?" "There are four Mr. President." "Where is the Seventh Fleet presently?"

"Sir right here, off the southwest coast of Sumatra." "Well Admiral, maybe we should have them move west. How do the rest of you feel?" "Admiral Timm, your thoughts."

"Mr. President, I think we have little choice, given what they appear to be doing."

"General Andrews, how many aircraft do we have in Turkey and Pakistan?"

"Four squadrons Mr. President; the Air Force is ready to respond if so ordered."

"Let me be clear gentlemen, the last thing we need is to start a war; nevertheless, we need to send them a message, the United States will respond, if needed, to protect American and allied interests.

I'll be talking to the Russian Ambassador and the Russian President about this matter. For now, I want the military to remain on standby; take no action except to reposition, unless I order it. Is everyone clear on that? Good, I'll have the Defense Secretary draw up the papers. Admiral Timm can I see you for a moment?"

"Admiral, I want you to insure everyone understands my order, there'll be no overt action, unless I say otherwise."

"Mr. President, consider it done." "Admiral, join me for lunch?"

"Okay."

"Admiral, have you spoke to your wife?"

"She said if that's what I want, it's fine with her."

"Okay, what have you decided, or haven't you decided?"

"Sir, I'm leaning towards retirement; I need to spend time with my family."

"Admiral, the country needs a man like you."

"Mr. President, I'm not sure you want a person like me, given some of the things I've done in the past."

Admiral, everyone has done something they later regret." "I know have."

Then it dawned on me, the Admiral is trying to tell me something, without saying so. Did he play a role in the President's death; or did he instruct the Secret Service not to look after my family, especially Lynn; she's most at risk.

"Well, Admiral Timm, enjoy retirement."

"Mr. President, thank you; by the way, I think Admiral Henry will make a good successor; you know, as vice chair, he'll assume my duties once I leave and do so until a successor is named."

"Thanks for the reminder."

In hindsight, if Admiral Timm was involved, I have further issues to deal with besides finding a replacement him, and many will have to be let go. I also have doubts about Robert's loyalty, but if I ask him to leave who would I appoint to take his place; Under Secretary of State Scanlan might be a possibility; best to think it over, at least for a while.

Time to start writing my speech; so much to talk about, in such a short time. It's going to be a challenge. I must keep it simple, if possible.

"Mrs. Witt, please contact the Press Secretary and have him to come to my office."

"Martin, clear everything off your schedule for the next thirty-six hours, I want you to help me with my presentation. I'll see you here in an hour."

What should I work on first, my Power-Point or the speech? Martin can prepare the data and the photo slides; I'll focus on the text, now to draft it.

Good evening my fellow Americans, the past nine days have been heartfelt for all of us. It all started with the untimely death of President Leonard, and then came the earthquake in the Mississippi River Valley, followed by a massive quake in the Middle East. However, before discussing that one, I want to take a minute to talk about the one that occurred here.

First, I'd like to thank the governors of Arkansas, Kentucky, Missouri, and Tennessee for all their hard work in coordinating their disaster response with the Office of Emergency Management. Second, I'd like to thank the Department of the Army and the National Guard, for their search and rescue efforts. Next, I'd like to thank all the businesses who supplied food, equipment and medicine. Finally, I'd like to thank the doctors, nurses, paramedics, firefighters, police, and volunteers; we couldn't have done it without you. When disaster strikes, that's when you know the true character of your

people. I couldn't prouder, I owe you all a debt
of thanks. To all the citizens directly affected by
the quake, please accept my heartfelt sympathy.
We'll do everything humanly possible to help
you rebuild your lives. Now I'd like to talk
about the Middle East.

The earthquake that struck that region was the
largest and most devastating quake that man has
ever seen. My thoughts and prayers go out to all
the victims and their families. This disaster
could well change their way of life, and for that
matter ours as well, and possibly the rest of the
world. Whenever a disaster like this happens,
chaos will result. I'm sure you're aware the U.S.
is heavily dependent on foreign oil, mostly from
the Middle East. Scientists tell me that supply
may not be available a time, as much as two
years, perhaps. If that isn't bad enough,
whatever remains may prove unusable, due to
molten contamination.

As such, we must make some tough decisions, now and tomorrow, given the affect such circumstances will have on our economy and our capital resources. After talking with a host of experts, I've decided to take immediate action to stabilize the situation before matters grow worse. As such Executive Order 031618 is now in effect.

This Order suspends Wall Street trading for five trading days, subject to an extension, if conditions warrant. I also suspended all monetary transfers and other capital resource transfers between banks and other financial intuitions (i.e., ones located outside the United States). In addition, the Order halts the exporting of finished gasoline and other refined petroleum products for an indeterminate amount of time. Finally, the Order freezes the price of crude and refined oil (e.g. gasoline, diesel, and motor oil) for five business days, subject to extension if warranted. I know these are drastic measures; I've received lots of criticism for ordering them, but I feel they were in the best interests of the nation, given what transpired. Since issuing the Order, business and congressional leaders and myself have begun the process of preparing long range plans.

Unfortunately, the plans will not return everything back to the way it was; nature made that impossible. Also, the solutions we've developed aren't simple, there are no quick fixes, however if we work hard, the opportunities they afford could prove endless.

Now I'd like to step you through key provisions of the plan. Keep in mind as you follow along, the Congress, the auto industry, and the major petroleum companies and refineries have collectively agreed to the plans we've adopted.

Well that seems like a good 'first' draft; nevertheless, I'll begin the editing process in a day or two.

"Mrs. Witt what is it?

"Mr. President the FBI Director is here and needs to speak with you right away."

"Well, have him come in, and when Martin shows up, tell him to wait."

"Director, what can I do for you?"

"I just heard about the foul up at the Secret Service headquarters; Ericson usually runs a tight ship."

"Director, that wasn't a little mix-up, I consider it a major blunder given all that has happened over the past week."

"Sir, I don't blame you for feeling that way."

"Maybe a little house cleaning is in order."

"What do you want me to do?"

"I want you to give me some names I should consider for the job."

"Does that mean you plan to fire Ericson?"

"That depends what he writes in his report, which by the way is due about now. If he chooses not to deliver it personally, I'll fire him on the spot. If he delivers it directly, I'll wait to read it before making my decision. I want you to read to."

"Sir, do you think that's a good idea; Ericson and I are friends and we go way back."

"Director I want you to know his rational for not protecting my children and grandchildren, and my sister-in-law. Did you know, I specifically told Director Ericson to insure her protection, given the sensitive nature of her work?"

"Mr. President, the report you wanted is here." "How did it come?" "Sir, Ericson delivered it." "If he's still here, please show him in."

"Mr. Ericson you know Director Bonds; have a seat. Would you care to summarize your findings? Let's start with my sister-in-law." "Mr. President, I misunderstood the nature of your request."

"I'm not sure what that means, explain it to me."

"I believe, based on the law, you lack the authority to issue an order of protection."

"Sir, that may or may not be true, but I do have an obligation to protect her, given the nature of her work for the government. Must I remind you, President Leonard died suddenly, and for no apparent reason? The First Lady, the Attorney General, and I collectively decided an immediate autopsy of the President was in order. My sister-in-law came here, at my request, because she's an expert pathologist and internist. I also felt someone from outside of Washington would help ensure ethical standards are followed throughout the procedure. It's not your job to second guess me."

"Isn't that right Director Bonds?"

"Ericson I'm afraid so."

"Mr. Ericson besides that, what was the hang up regarding my children and grandchildren and who was the clown posing as one of your agents? Were you aware he was trying to enter my daughter house?" "I'm waiting."

"Mr. President, I thought I issued an order of protection but apparently something happen to my directive."

"When did you issue it?"

"I think it was Monday; the day of the funeral."

"Tell me Mr. Ericson, when did I become President?"

"Sir, Thursday, February 29."

"Why did you wait until Monday, did you think my family would be okay without protection?"

"Mr. President, it's been a difficult week for all."

"What do we know about the man posing as a federal agent, is he in custody, if not, why not?"

"Sir, the local police turned him over to one of my agents approximately an hour after we were told of his presence."

"So where is he now?"

"We questioned the suspect, and then turned him over to the FBI."

"Bonds, do your boys have him?"

"Mr. President, I don't know, let me make a call."

"Ericson, your actions or should I say lack of them are unconscionable, borderline criminal."

"Mr. President, we don't have him, never did."

"So, where is he?"

"We don't know."

"Let's find him, now. Ericson you're fired, effective immediately. Director Bonds, take Mr. Ericson into custody, pending an investigation and possible charges for dereliction of duty. I want the FBI to investigate this matter, and Mr. Bonds I want you to personally verify that every member of my family has around the clock protection. Also, I want the Deputy Director of the FBI to head the Secret Service until I pick a replacement. That's it; now get him out of here."

"Martin, come in, we have work to do."

"Mr. President, what was that?"

"Only a little housekeeping, that's all. Now, do you have all the data you need for the slides?"

"Yes."

"Read my initial draft and tell me what you think. I want an honest opinion not just something you think I want to hear. Pay attention to tone; also, whether any portion is condescending in any way. While you're doing that, I need to make some calls."

"Mr. Speaker, John Keller, do you have a few minutes. Tomorrow night I'd like you, Senator Roth, and perhaps an auto executive to join me in the Oval Office while I deliver my closing remarks. We need to show the public that government and the captains of industry can and will work together to get things done."

"Can I count on you?"

"Yes."

"Senator Roth, John Keller, do you have a few minutes? I just spoke to the Speaker and he agreed to join me in the Oval Office at the conclusion of my speech. I'd like you there as well. Can I count on you?"

"Yes."

"That's great; I'll see you tomorrow night. Oh, one thing more, which auto exec should we invite? I'd like you to make the choice; you know most."

"Martin, are you finished?"

"Yes Mr. President."

"Well, tell me, what you think?"

"Sir, overall it's an excellent draft, although I did jot down a few suggestions. We can go over them now or wait until we're done with the PowerPoint."

"Let's work on the presentation first; that'll take the most time. Here's an outline of the points we need to cover."

"First, we have to identify where we get our crude oil and natural gas supplies from, along with the proportional percentage each contributes to our overall total, up until the time of the quake.

Second, I want to show how those various sources are presently consumed; for example: by private autos, buses, trucks, rail, planes, etc.

Third, I want to identify how each entity will be affected by supply losses as a result of the quake.

Fourth, I want to show the financial impact the loss will have on each entity, on a typical business, on a typical family.

Fifth, I want to identify the opportunities open to us given the events that have occurred.

Sixth, I want to show how each opportunity benefits each entity. Seven, I want to explain the upfront costs and the timeline necessary to achieve full implementation.

Finally, I want to identify all the players, and their specific roles in the process. The package could be a tough sell; but we have few options. In addition, we have to sell it as a long-term proposition. If we do, the country may again achieve energy independence. I ask you, what greater contribution is there, for our children and grandchildren. The possibilities could be endless. So Martin, what do you think? Do we have all the necessary data to put the presentation together?"

"Yes sir, I think we do. However, I suggest we have a PowerPoint expert help design the slides."

"Do you have someone in mind?"

"Yes, I can personally vouch for him; and he can keep things to himself."

"Good, get him over here so he can get to work. Here is my review of your analysis and data sets; I've highlighted the items that I believe are most relevant. The two of you can work on putting it all together, now I have to figure out what to do with the Russians; but I'm available for questions."

"Mr. Ambassador, President Keller when can we sit down for a chat, things seem to be getting out of hand. I know what you said when you left my office the other day. Would later this afternoon work out?"

"That'll work Mr. President." "Fine, see you then."

I think the Russians are putting me to the test (i.e., to see how far they can push me before I push back). If needed, I can be just as pushy. A few Congressmen, some Senators and a few staffers know that all too well. I have neither the time nor the patience for any kind of nonsense.

"Mr. President, the FBI Director is on the phone."

"Director Bonds thanks for getting back to me. Is the security detail in place, I no longer want to worry about my family's safety?"

"They are safe sir."

"Great, how about my sister-in-law, is she safe?"

"She is."

"One more thing, I want you to expedite your investigation of the Secret Service; if heads have to roll, so be it. Also, I'll be flying to Minnesota in the morning, to spend a day alone with my family. I know I mentioned the trip to Ericson, but I'm not sure he passed the information along. Would you mind checking on it? Call if you need something."

"Mr. President, the Russian Ambassador is here."

"Please show him in."

"Mr. Ambassador thanks for coming; have a seat. We need to talk about the Middle East situation. What's Russia's position regarding the region?"

"Mr. President, our position hasn't changed; because of President Leonard's death or because of the devastating quake that occurred there, our foreign policy remains the same." "With all due respect Mr. Ambassador, I don't believe you. I think Russia sees these events as an opportunity to

243

expand its influence. If you think I'm going to sit back and ignore the obvious, you're mistaken. Over the next couple of years, the Middle East will be very unstable, even more than it is now; what we don't need is a super-power making matters worse. I think it is imperative we agree on how we can work together. Next month, both our countries will attend the World Economic Conference in Paris; I think it's vital the Russian President and I sit down and work through the issues, with the hope of reaching some consensus concerning the Middle East. Mr. Ambassador, I'd like you to discuss this matter with your President and get him to agree to a meeting. Can you do that?"

"Mr. President, the only thing I'll promise you, I'll talk to him. Now I'd like to ask you a question. What's your Navy doing in the Middle East?"

"Why Mr. Ambassador, nothing more than what Russia seems to be doing; we're looking out for our interests; that should come as no surprise."

"Well Mr. President, I think we've both said enough." "I agree, thanks for coming. Oh, by the way that was an interesting comment you made, as you were leaving my office the other day."

The Ambassador now seems confused, you should see the look on his face; maybe he got the message. Time will tell if I'm right.

"Mr. President. Mr. Roberts is here, and wants to talk to you."

"Come in Wayne, I can give you a few minutes."

"Mr. President we need to talk about the Congressional vote.

"Sir, I think you're getting ahead of yourself; I think you should wait and see what develops."

"So, what should I do about my Executive Order?"

"Rescind it."

"Well Wayne I find your comments quite interesting; I just don't agree with them. We don't have the luxury of sitting around and doing nothing. The coming days will be unsettling, even with my plan. Implementation could also take up to a year; and perhaps another for significant relief. Americans are impatient, they want things done right now, but change of this magnitude will take time. Wayne, I didn't create these problems; that is, our heavy reliance on oil imports nor the Middle East quake, but I have to deal with them just the same. If you don't agree with my choices, maybe you should find another job. I need people who will support my position, not undermine them.

Wayne is that your intent?"

"No sir, I don't think so."

"Well that's good."

Sadly, I don't believe him; his eyes tell a different story. I hope he resigns, if not I'll fire him.

"Martin, how are you doing?" "Are your graphs comprehensive but yet simple enough to understand?"

"They are."

Don't forget to highlight and compare total crude oil usage, total import usage, and Persian Gulf import usage in 2011 with our present usage distribution, utilizing the same categories."

"Sir, we have."

"Also, I'd like to highlight category distribution once the plan is in place for two years." "Mr. President, I think we have everything covered."

"How long before you finalize it?

"We should have it done by this evening."

"That's fine; I'll finish my comments in the morning."

"Have the networks given us airtime tomorrow evening?"

"Yes, they have, we're set for 8:00."

"How long will the presentation take?"

"I'm guessing, no more than twenty minutes. I don't want to bore anyone."

"That's a good idea."

"Thanks Martin, I just hope Congress does its job."

"Sir, Senator Olson is returning your call."

"Mark thanks for getting back to me; I'd like you to join me for dinner, there are few things I need to discuss with you. Sure, bring your wife, besides she's better looking than you, no offense. Professor Johnson, I thought she went home. She did, why is she back so soon? Book deal, well that explains it. Okay, bring her along, but I have to tell you, she makes me a little nervous; maybe because I can't figure her out, but then I haven't had much practice as of late, not that it would make any difference. Have to go now, the Head of NBC News is on the other line; see you at 7:00."

"Mr. Mills, what can I do for you?"
"Mr. President, NBC News would like an inclusive interview on the problems that came about as a result of the Middle East quake; we'd like to do it tomorrow, if that's possible."

"Mr. Mills tomorrow is out of the question. However, I could do it Sunday morning aboard Air Force One; I'm flying home to visit my family for the day. If that works for you, your crew has to be at Andrews by 5:30, at the latest. Also call Mrs. Witt with the names of your reporters. Who is the lead reporter?

Tom Allen; good choice, he's a fine journalist. One thing more, I'd like a list of subject areas beforehand; there are areas I don't wish to discuss."

"No problem."

"When will the piece air?" "Next week I believe."

"Mr. Mills, I'd prefer if it runs as soon as possible, but no later than next Friday."

"Mr. President we can discuss that later."

"Mr. Mills, I don't mean to cut you off, but I have to go; I have lots to do, and my guests are here."

"Mark, come in. Betty, as always, nice to see you; Professor Johnson, Mary, this is a pleasant surprise. Would anyone care for drink? The usually, Mary what would you like?" "I'll have the same." "Please sit down everyone and relax; dinner is set for 7:30, so we have time to talk."

"So, Mark, what've you heard on Capitol Hill?"

"Mr. President, nothing out of the ordinary, the usual whining and crying, same old stuff."

"That's fine, but what about the plan I sent them to vote on tomorrow, who are the naysayers?"

"Well, you may already know who they are from your time on Capitol Hill."

"Do you think Senator Roth can muster enough votes to get it passed?"
"Yes, I believe so; rumor has it passing by 2 to 1; now the House is another story."

"You know I've never been a fan of the Speaker; I think he's a blowhard, all mouth and no action. How hard should I push him, or should I talk directly to the doubters?"

"Mr. President, I'd suggest a little of each; you know those oil states are going to be a tough nut to crack; they think Washington should get the hell out of the way and let them do as they please."

"You mean a fox standing guarding the hen house."

"Well sort of like that."

"Mark, I want to ask you something very personal."

"Ask away."

"As you know, I must appoint someone to the Office of Vice President, someone that can get through confirmation without being torn apart. I'm open to suggestions, including Mark Olson."
"Mr. President, I'm flattered by your offer, I'm sure I can come up with a few names; I'm not sure I'd make a good candidate." "Betty, what would you think if Mark was VP?" "John, Mr. President, I'd call it a giant step backwards, Mark loves the Senate, and I love being a Senator's wife."

"You know, you might be right, but there's no harm in asking. In any case, I'd like to submit a name sometime within the next two weeks."

"Professor Johnson, I'm sorry I have ignored you, unfortunately there are times when Presidential affairs come before personal pleasantries."

"Mark tells me you came back to Washington to sign a book deal." "Yes Mr. President, one of my former publishers agreed to market my book."

"I'm looking forward to reading it when it's done."

"I can send you a signed copy if you wish."

"That would be nice."
"Mr. President, I have a favor to ask."

"Go ahead."

"Betty says you are an accomplished pianist, especially with classical pieces."

"She's being overly kind."

"Well I'd like to hear you play, if you don't mind; I understand you know several Beethoven works."

"I guess we have a few minutes before dinner, how about Moonlight Sonata."

"That would be nice."

You know I really shouldn't be playing this one, my wife loved the piece and whenever I played it, she would get romantic; it is peaceful though, and I

sure can use that. I'll let the music speak for itself.
As I'm nearing the end, I mistakenly look up for a
moment, I then saw my wife standing by the piano.
Then I realize its Mary Louise, and she to, has that
same look on her face, it's frightening, although I
admit I love it.

"Soups on, let's eat." During dinner, everyone
exchanges pleasantries and talk about our days back
in Minnesota. Mary smiles often but says little.

Then, as I'm about to leave the table, Betty comes
over and whispers to me,

"You know, I think she likes you."

"I don't know what to say, really, are you sure?"

If that wasn't bad enough, Mary then comes over
and gives me a big hug; I feel the goose bumps
running down my back. Then she looks straight at
me, in that professor stance of hers.

"Mr. President we need to talk."

Day 10

Saturday, March 9 2:35 am

Getting to sleep proves difficult; I kept waking up
thinking about the tone I should use when I present
my plan. When I resolved that, another issue
popped up and took its place. Now the phone, am I
dreaming; I'll ignore it; still the ringing continues.
I'm going to take that darn receiver off the hook.
However, as I pick it up, a loud voice says, Mr.
President, Mr. President.

"Yes, what is it?"

"Sir, this is the Defense Secretary, I need you to
come to the Situation Room immediately."

The CIA had just confirmed that Israel was
planning to launch a massive air strike on Syria.
Christ, that's the last thing we need; then everything
will go to hell; and I'm sure Russians will be more
than willing to jump in and help. If that happens,
Israel will want us to defend her.

"Mr. Secretary get the Israel Prime Minister on the phone, I'll meet you in the Situation Room in 15 minutes; also make sure the Joint Chiefs and someone from Central Intelligence are there. I want to know who created this mess."

Then I was handed a recently prepared report about the situation.

Early last evening, the CIA intercepted a Syrian message stating they had arrested six Israeli officials and their families. They intend to hold them hostage. Apparently, their plane had to make an emergency landing in Syria; how the Syrian military knew Israeli officials and their families were on board remains a mystery; we believe the incident was no accident, they planned all along. As technicians worked on the plane, the Syrian police stormed the aircraft and arrested all the Israelis and their families. Initially, we weren't sure the reason for the siege. However, just minutes ago, Syria reportedly told Israel that unless they release all Syrian prisoners, the hostages will be shot, one every hour, if demands are not met. That includes family members. Israel's response, "we don't negotiate with terrorists". I need to make a call.

"Mr. Prime Minister, President Keller. Minutes ago, I was informed of your situation, I'm sympathetic, but we must not turn it into an armed conflict; the region is already unstable enough from the quake. If you engaged an air strike, the Russians will likely respond in support of Syria, and if that happens, it's no telling where it might lead. The best course, in my view, would be to let my people talk with the Russians and see if we could resolve the situation. I know you think Syria is trying to push you around, they are, but you also need to consider the bigger picture. In the end, mass casualties serve no one."

"Will you let us negotiate on your behalf?"

"Okay Mr. President."

"Thank you; I'll get the State Department on it."

Now off to the Situation Room.

"Listen up everyone; you heard what I told the Prime Minister. Defense, maintain your position and stand by. State get in touch with the Russians, I want hourly progress reports, and keep Defense informed; CIA keep monitoring for further developments, report them directly to me; and Staff you're going to help them carry out my directives. Let's get to work."

Now I must call the governors regarding this morning's congressional vote.

"Mr. President, I have the governors of California, Texas, Oklahoma, New York, and Ohio standing by, via satellite."

"Governors, good morning thanks for taking my call. In a couple of hours, Congress will vote on a major piece of legislation that will define this country's energy future, with respect to transportation. As you know, we've been far too dependent on Middle East oil, and been unwilling to make major changes to reduce or eliminate such dependency. Nature now, has forced us to change. I've consulted with the oil and auto industries and Congressional leaders about the course we need to take. Together we must develop a Plan that addresses the issues head on; and if it's successful, future economic prospects, will be much improved. I've called you together to ask for your support."

"The Plan is not a government giveaway; those plans work only as long as the money holds out; our plan doesn't work that way. I'm asking private industry to help implement our new energy strategy. Industry will receive interest free loans, in the form of tax credits, once specific benchmarks are met.

So where is the money coming from? We're proposing a two cent per gallon tax on all liquid fuels and two and half cent tax per cubic foot on gaseous fuels (e.g. natural gas and hydrogen). This tax will be dropped once the credits are recouped."

"I know all of you personally, and I think you know me well enough, that I don't play games. In the next few minutes each of you will be receiving the final draft of the plan, the draft Congress will vote on later this morning. I'm available to answer any questions you might have."

"Mr. President. Governor Smith, we'll get back to you on that."

"Fellows thanks for your time."

"Mr. President, FBI Director Bonds is waiting to talk to you."

"Show him in Mrs. Witt."

"Director what can I do for you?"

"Mr. President, I just received word the First Lady had received a package from an import company just two days before the President's death." "So what's so strange about that?"

"Well as it turns out, the company name printed on the package doesn't exist, it's bogus."

"Do we know where it came from?"

"Not exactly, all we know is it came from Italy."

"Do you think he had something to do with the President's death?"

"It could be; for now, it's only a lead."

"Did you ask the First Lady about it?"

"No, I wanted to wait until we have more information; I'd like to know what was in the package before I start asking a lot of questions."

"I think that's wise, keep me posted; good work."

Now where did I put the Speaker's phone number; oh, here it is.

"Mr. Speaker, John Keller how are things looking this morning?"

"Great, things are shaping up; only a few naysayers to deal with."

"Where does the vote stand right now?"

"It looks like 241 to 194; to approve, but we'll try to get more onboard."

"Have you spoken to Senator Roth this morning?"

"No, but I plan to when I'm done talking to you."

"You better; I heard a rumor he' in trouble."

"Mr. Speaker thanks for the heads up; what time is the vote?"

"11:30; I'll call with the results."

Now to call Roth and find out the hold up.

"Senator Roth, how are you today?"

"Good."

"How's the vote shaping up in the Senate, I heard a rumor you were having some trouble?"

"I bet the Speaker told you that, he's always trying to stir things up."

"Senator is it true, are you having problems?"

"No sir, we aren't."

"So, where does the vote stand now?"

"The vote, 56 for, 41 opposed and 2, undecided."

"Do you think it'll hold up in the next vote?"

"Yes; I'll call you when I know the results."

"Great, I'll be expecting your phone call."

Now I need time to relax. I'll feel better once the vote is over; I also need time to review my speech for tonight; forty-five minutes later the phone rings.

"Mr. Speaker, it's nice to hear your voice."

"Mr. President the House did it, the vote 249 to 187, one abstained. I can't say the same in the Senate."

"At the last minute, the junior Senator from Kansas decided to filibuster, so until he sits down the Senate cannot call the question."

"Mr. Speaker, don't worry I'll take care of that; thanks for all your help."

"Mrs. Witt, get the Governor of Kansas on the phone, I need to speak with him."

"Governor, John Keller, we have a problem. It seems your junior Senator is delaying an important vote with his filibuster. Sir, this vote is vital to the country; we can't have a hot dog holding up the process simply to appease his right-wing supporters. Apparently, he doesn't realize how much aid Kansas receives, maybe you should remind him."

"Mr. President, if I take care of that, are we even?"
"Yes, and I assure you Kansas won't be forgotten."

Just to make sure, I'm going to visit the Senate.

"Mrs. Witt have the Secret Service bring my car around, I'll be at the Capitol for a while."

It's only been two weeks since I last visited; though it seems like months. If I stay in the back of the chamber, maybe no one will notice I'm there. I see the junior Senator from Kansas has taken his seat. The President Pro-Tem is about to call the question. The vote, 65 in favor, 38 oppose, with two abstentions; the bill passes. Now I feel better.

As I ready to leave, I hear a loud shout, "The President is here." Now I can't leave; I need to thank these folks and House members as well. It's a good thing a draft of tonight's presentation is completed; I won't have time to work anymore.

"Senators the country thanks you, I thank you; Washington has come together in a time of need."

Now I'm going for a walk, think about my speech and then have supper. Then the time arrives.

"Mr. President, we have to do a sound check."

"I'll be there in a minute; I'm making some last-minute changes."

"Do you want me at my desk; I've never done a live presentation from the White House?

"Sir, seated at your desk will be just fine."

I feel like a teenager about to meet his girlfriend's parents for the first time; waiting is stressful.

"Fellows, how is my hair, my tie?"

"You look great, just have a seat, we're on in two."

"Good evening my fellow Americans, I come before you tonight to discuss some important issues. I don't need to tell you how traumatic the past ten days have been. First the unexpected death of President Leonard, then the earthquake in our country, followed by a massive quake in the Middle East. However, before I delve into that disaster, I want to take a minute to talk about ours. To start,

I'd like to thank the governors of Arkansas, Kentucky, Missouri, and Tennessee for all their hard work in coordinating the disaster response with the Office of Emergency Management. Second, I'd like to thank the Department of the Army, particularly the National Guard, for all their efforts with search and rescue. Third, I wish to thank all the businesses that supplied food, equipment and medicine. Last of all, I want to thank the doctors, nurses, paramedics, firefighters, police, and volunteers; we couldn't have done it without your help. When a disaster strikes, that's when we see the true character of America. I couldn't be more proud of this group; we are in your debt. To all the good men and women who were directly affected by the earthquake, please accept my heartfelt sympathy. We will do everything humanly possible to help you rebuild. Now I'd like to focus your attention on the Middle East."

"The earthquake that struck the Middle East was the largest and most devastating quake that man has ever seen. My thoughts and prayers go out to all the people living in that region. A way of life could change, perhaps forever, not only in the affected region but around the world. Whenever a disaster of this magnitude occurs, chaos and confusion will likely ensure."

"For the past half century, this country grew dependent on foreign oil; some of it from the Middle East Region. Geologists in this country now tell me that supply might not be available for a long time; even worse, some of those supplies might have been rendered useless due to molten contamination. Major decisions needed to be made, given the scope of the disaster. The outcomes of that disaster will affect our way of life, our economy, and our financial resources. After consulting with several leaders, I decided we must do everything possible to stabilize matters and do so immediately before things got worse and/or irreversible."

"Therefore, I took the first step in issuing Executive Order 031618. The Order suspends Wall Street trading, for five trading days, subject to an extension if conditions warrant. Second, it suspends all monetary transfers and other capital resources with banks and other financial entities located outside the United States. Third, it halts the export of all finished gasoline and other refined petroleum products for an indeterminate amount of time. Fourth, it freezes the price of all crude and refined products (e.g. gasoline, diesel fuel, and motor oil) for five business days, subject to an extension."

"I know these are drastic measures, but I feel they were necessary, given what has transpired. Since issuing the order, business and congressional leaders and myself, have worked out a long-range plan. The solutions outlined in the plan, won't restore things as they were; nature has made that impossible. Nevertheless, the Plan will put us on track towards less dependence on foreign oil. The Plan is not a simple one, nor will its effects be immediate, but if we all work together, success will happen soon enough. Now I'd like to show you some graphic illustrations that represent what I've been talking about."

"Figure 1 indicates the number of barrels of crude oil we used in 2011, arranged by product category. Notice, nearly half of our per-day usage was gasoline (8.75 million barrels)."

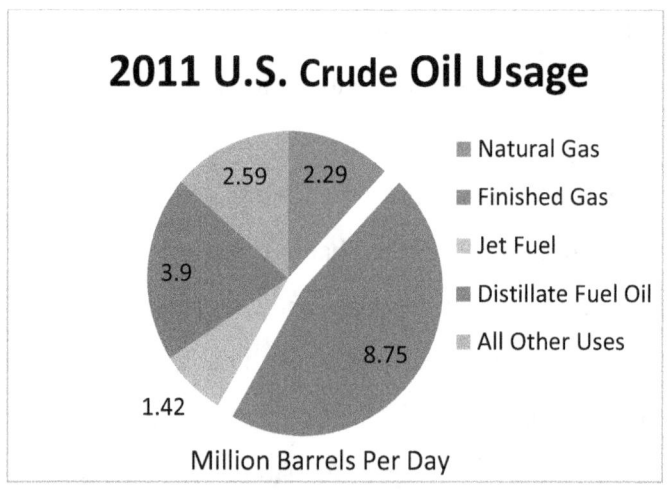

Figure 1

"Figure 2 illustrates where are usage is today, thru 2017. You'll notice overall, consumption has remained fairly constant, mostly by improving efficiency, especially in gasoline usage. Now let's look at how oil imports influence usage."

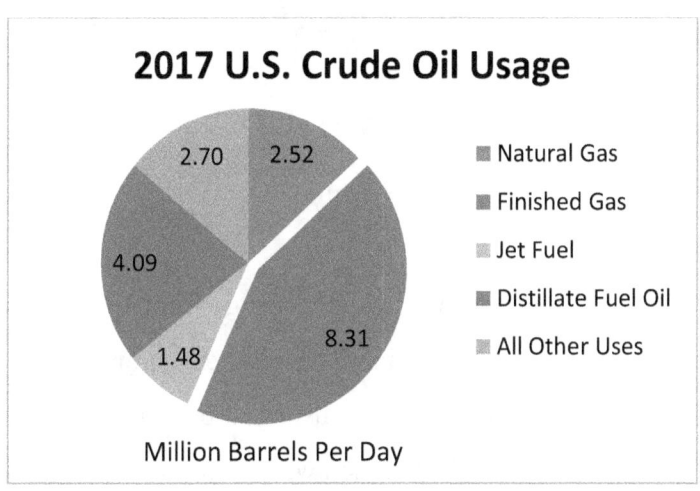

2017 U.S. Crude Oil Usage

2.70   2.52

4.09

1.48   8.31

- Natural Gas
- Finished Gas
- Jet Fuel
- Distillate Fuel Oil
- All Other Uses

Million Barrels Per Day

Figure 2

"In 2011, as Figure 3 illustrates, nearly half of our crude oil imports were used for gasoline (3.98 million barrels per day), 45% of 8.75 total; other categories are proportionately the same. Now let's compare that to today."

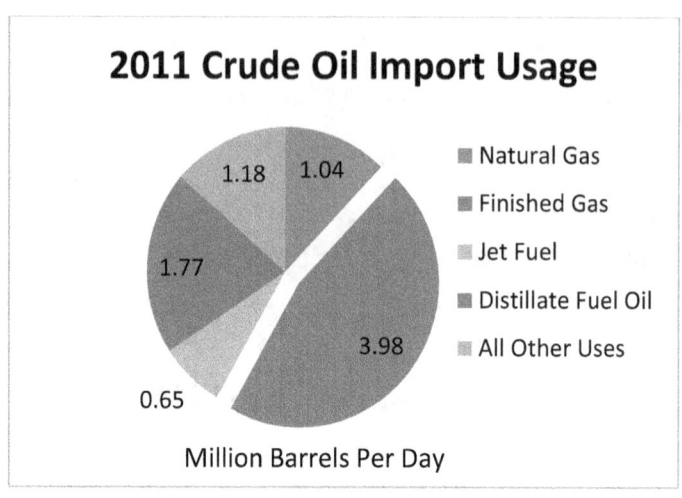

Figure 3

"As Figure 4 illustrates, the change from 2011 is proportional to the change in total consumption for the same time frame. I must point out, once foreign crude arrives; it's blended with domestic supplies. Now let's exam crude oil just from the Persian Gulf Region (the supplies now cut off)."

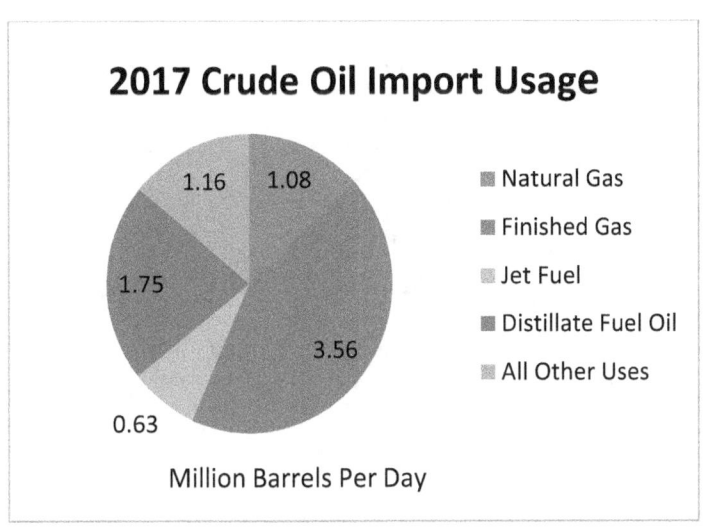

Figure 4

"In 2011, as Figure 5 illustrates, about 46 percent (.79 /1.7 mpd) of Persian Gulf supplies was refined into gasoline. Although not illustrated, 2011 crude oil import totals approached 8.6 million barrels per day and of that amount approximately 15 percent or 1.3 million barrels was from the Persian Gulf, by December 2017, that amount changed significantly."

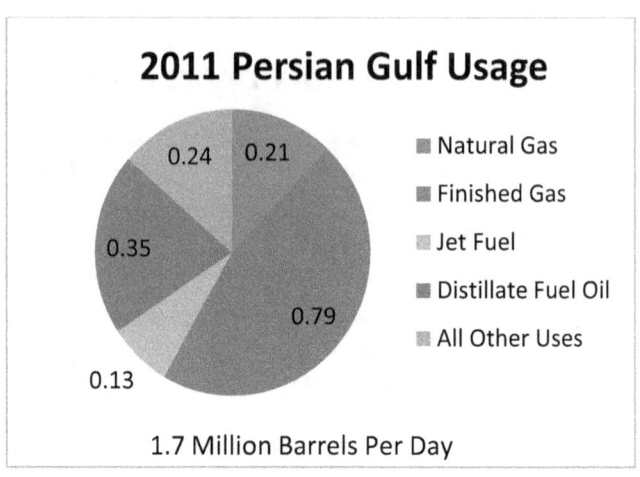

Figure 5

"As you see, by comparing 2017 totals in Figure 6 to those from 2011, overall Persian Gulf imports went down about 6 percent; 1.7 to 1.6 million barrels per day. Presently, only about 9 percent of our OVERALL crude oil needs comes from the Persian Gulf. However, that source is now cut off, for an undetermined amount of time. As such, we assume they're lost forever."

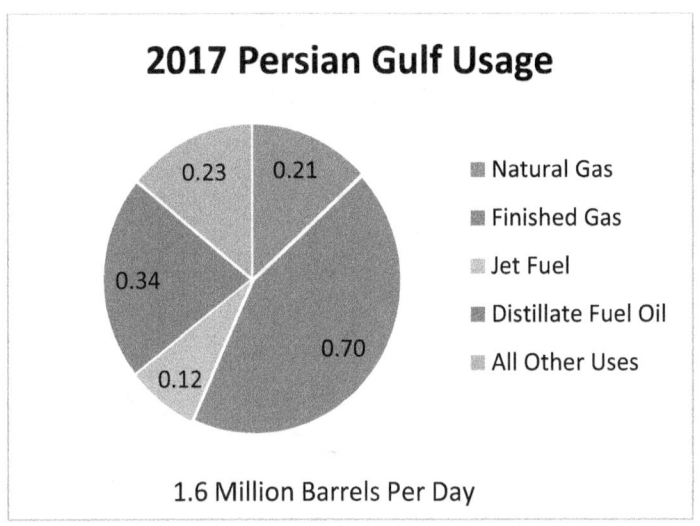

Figure 6

"The plan the Congress, the business community and I, collectively, developed addresses that situation, however, elements of the Plan will take up to two years to fully implement. Figure 7 illustrates current and anticipated need from all sources, assuming nine percent of our total supply is completely lost. The Congress, the business community and I all agree the Plan is doable. If we fail to act, the price of crude and finished gasoline will increase dramatically, and cause an economic disaster. Now let's look at the Plan's tenets."

275

Present and Projected Crude Oil Sources by Percentage

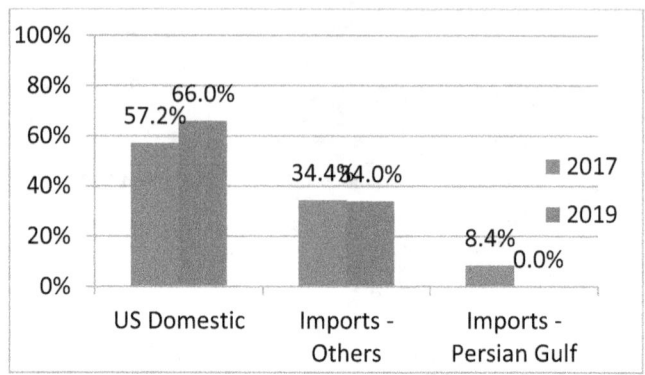

Figure 7

"The Plan, as proposed, is based on the following considerations, as we know them:

> The price of crude oil and gasoline will increase dramatically, without action
>
> Finding other affordable sources of crude oil will become very difficult
>
> Overall petroleum consumption must be reduced through greater efficiencies
>
> The long term supply of Natural Gas is excellent and should be utilized

Hydrogen fuel technology is at a point where it can be used safely in vehicles

The automobile industry can now produce engines that use natural gas or hydrogen for the same cost as gasoline units

Virtually all cars and most light pickups produced in the last two years can be converted to natural gas or hydrogen, at a modest cost, and done in only a few days

Natural Gas and hydrogen offer at least a 25 percent greater efficiency compared to gasoline vehicles of the same size

Commercial vehicles, primarily buses, can be converted to use natural gas or hydrogen

Fueling stations at present are not able to handle new fuels and must be upgraded

Producing alternative fuel vehicles and converting older ones and upgrading fueling stations across the country will take up to two years to complete.

The Congress will provide incentives to the automotive industry, the oil industry and all associated filling stations across the country so as to expedite the conversion process as quickly and as cost effectively as possible"

"As you can see, the Plan is quite comprehensive. I believe it will give us our best chance to meet our energy needs well into the future. It will however, require cooperation and patience. Over the next two years, there will be great progress, but setbacks will occur. Also, some people may try to exploit the situation for their own benefit; I understand that and will deal with it. That's why I need everyone's cooperation. Events have forced us to face reality, we have to the fix it ourselves, nobody is going to do it for us. My job, as President, is to lead the nation, and set a positive course for the future. I can't do it alone; I need your help."

"As of 12:01 am this Tuesday, Executive Order 031618 is rescinded; trading on Wall Street will be allowed to resume; banks can also resume capital transfers; the band on fuel exports is also lifted.

However, I am extending the freeze on crude oil and gasoline prices for another seven days in order to assess the condition of our financial markets."

"We must work together as one America, not one mirrored in conflict and chaos. This is about the future, the future of our children and grandchildren. I hope we can set aside our differences and get the job done. We must and we will. Thank you for your attention, good evening."

I'm glad that's over with; I'm exhausted. Did I say enough, did I say too much? Did I give the impression I was in charge, and did they believe me? I guess I can't change that now. Still, do they truly believe the man from Minnesota has what it takes to be Commander and Chief? I never prepared for this job nor did I ever expect to have it. Destiny, I guess decided for me.

Suddenly, my moment of self-indulgence evaporates. It seems a small mob has taken over the

Oval Office, there's hollering, pushing and shoving. What do they want?

"Mr. President, you gave a fantastic speech."

"Thank you, Mr. Speaker; and thank the Congress for all its hard work"

"Martin, what do you need?"

"I have the network summaries; do you want to review them now?"

"Not especially, I should talk to these people, don't you think? Anyway, I know what Fox is going to say, I think the other networks and cable news will support us, but you never know about the news folks; sometimes it's more about creating drama than reporting the facts. Go ahead put them on my desk; I'll look at them later."

"Senator Roth, good of you to come. Did the heads of the big three come with you?"

"No sir, but they'll probably be here shortly but I think the fellows from Honda and Toyota are somewhere in the room." "Thanks for the info."

"Mr. Oher, it's nice to see you. Would you mind introducing your associates?"

"No not all; Mr. President, this is William Davis from General Motors; Fred Arnett President from Ford; Lee Evans from Chrysler; Ross Fredricks President of Honda America; and David Chao from Toyota America."

"Men it's certainly nice to meet you, thank you for coming. I'm looking forward to talking to each one of you separately. Now if you'll excuse me, I have a few more people I need to speak to before they leave. Director Bonds, do you have a minute?"

"Director forgive me, I've forgotten the name of your Assistant."

"Mr. President, his name is Peter Yates."

"That's right, now I remember." "Have you told him about his temporary assignment, as Head of the Secret Service?"

"I did this morning, Pete is looking forward to it, you know he started out in the Secret Service before switching to the FBI. He does have a question." He wants to know if he can ride along with you on Air Force; he needs to talk over some things."

"Sure, that's fine; tell him to be at Andrews by 5:45, we leave promptly at 6:00."

"Sir, he'll be there, I can assure you, by the way, great presentation."

"Thank you, sir." "Amanda, what is it?"

"Your daughter has been trying to reach you."

Whoops, I forgot to call, I'll do it now.

"Honey, how are you, is everything alright?"

"Yes Dad, everything is fine. I just wanted to make sure you were coming tomorrow; the kids are really looking forward to seeing 'Papa'."

"Yes, we'll be land around 7:00, your time; but it could take a while to get to your house. Do you bake any of my favorites?"

"Yes Dad, yes Mr. President."

"Dad will do. Did you watch the speech?"

"David and I watched it together."

"Well what did you think?"

"Dad we thought it was excellent. Your presentation, through and complete. Very easy to follow, you were quite sincere."

"I don't mind telling you, I was nervous before, during and after, in fact I still haven't settled down completely."

"Dad, go play the piano; that should help."

"Thanks honey."

Well, one more round of hand shaking, then I'm off.

"Good night everyone; thanks for your support. Madam Secretary, Vickie, when you leave, could you ask my steward to fix me a sandwich and open a bottle of my favorite wine, he knows what I like. He can bring them to the Blue Room; I'll be at the piano, relaxing. Thanks."

"Mr. President, here is your order."

"Vickie, you didn't have to do that, the steward is on duty until ten."

"It was no trouble, I'm happy to do it."

"Sir, do you mind if I ask you a personal question?"

"Go ahead ask away." "Why haven't you married again, you're a good looking fellow?"

"You see Vickie, it comes down to subjectivity; it seems the women I meet have a different take. My wife and I were very close, and maybe finding someone to replace her didn't seem all that urgent, and maybe the women I came in contact sense that."

"How about you, did you ever get marry?"

"No, work has been my life, and I'm always on the go; relationships I have had, usually fall apart when I'm away."

"You know, you're a very attractive and very intelligent; I'm sure there's someone out there."

"Mr. President, this is getting heavy, maybe we should change the subject."

"Well you brought it up I didn't, and by the way, when we're alone, please call me John."

"Okay, John where did you learn to play the piano, the piece you're playing is beautiful?"

"I started playing in High School. At the time, I was recovering from a broken rib I sustained in the final football game of the year; the injury kept me from attending wrestling practice the following week, so on a bet with mom I took up the piano. After years of listening to her, it somehow wore off on me; I have played off and on ever since, mostly classical works."

"How about opera, how did that come about?"

"That came about purely by accident. As to how, I rather not talk about it. I prefer to play and yes sing be it in private, it's personal, just leave at that.

"Mr. President, John; I should be going; I've taken up too much of your time, but before I go, could I ask you one more question?"

"Vickie, I'm all ears."

"Do you we need a First Lady?"

"Madam are you inferring something?"

She simply smiles and then walks away, not uttering a word.

It's been a long day, I need some sleep, Marine One will be here to get at 5:30 (AM).

Sunday, March 10 4:30 am

By all accounts, yesterday was exceptional; everything went very well. So why do I feel on edge. Maybe I didn't get enough sleep, or maybe it's because I'm a cautious person by nature, maybe it's living in Washington. I'm going to take shower, have some juice and relax; after all, I'm going home to see my family. I need the break, if only for a day. Newspapers and briefs can wait until I get on the plane; but I best read them before my interview; I have to be prepared, in case something unfamiliar comes up. Now for some fresh air and watch the sunrise. It looks like a beautiful morning.

"Mr. President, Marine-One will be landing in five minutes. Are these the things you want taken along?"

"Yes, they are, be careful don't crush that large box; it has presents I promised the grandkids."

Off in the distance the sound of a helicopter; it's now passing over the Pentagon. I best get my briefcase; only I handle it. As soon as I'm aboard, we lift off. The ride is smooth; the view spectacular; and the sun, shining brightly. I feel relaxed, but a bit uneasy; did I overlook something. Try as I may, I can't figure out what maybe bothering me. As we land, I notice big blue a.k.a. Air Force One sitting there awaiting my arrival. As I step out, Air Force personnel and the Secret Service approach. When I look back in the other direction, I notice what appears to be a Secret Service agent standing by himself. He looks familiar; although I have a bad feeling about him.

If I remember right, he's the man who tried to get into my daughter's house; posing as a Secret Service agent. Instinctively, I told Elizabeth to take a picture of him and send it to me. I now open my phone to look at the picture, it's him alright.

"Mr. President, Peter Yates."

"Mr. Yates, good morning. Do you know that man standing over there?"

"No, not personally, but the former Director just reinstated him; apparently he had been on suspension."

"Do you know why?"

"I don't, why do you ask?"

"Look at the photo my daughter sent me; this is the same guy who tried to enter her house."

"Are you sure?"

"Go ahead look for yourself."

"What do you want me to do Mr. President?"

"I want you to arrest him, then conduct a thorough investigation as to his activities; and when you're finished, I want your report sent directly to me."

"Colonel David, I have reason to believe the plane's security has been compromised, what's the status of its twin mate?"

"Sir, it's available, it just needs to be fueled and a pre-flight inspection."

"Colonel how long will that take?"

"It should take no more than an hour."

"Get on it; my family is expecting me. Also, I want a full and complete inspection of this aircraft, top to bottom, understood."

"Understood."

"If anyone asks why we switched planes, tell them, it's at the President's request."

"Yes sir."

Seventy minutes later, we're airborne."

A quick scan of the morning paper reveals new concerns; They'll have to wait until I get back.

"Sir, the Air Force reports they found suspicious activity in the cargo hole. They did not elaborate."

"Thank you, Agent Johnson."

Now I have an important call to make.

"Let me speak to the Secretary of the Air Force. I don't care where he is; just get him on the phone."

Mr. Secretary, John Keller. No, I'm not okay. I was just told that our initial aircraft, the one I planned to use, has security issues; they tell me safety was compromised."

"I want you to conduct a full investigation into this matter and exercise oversight. I don't give a crap about military protocol; just get it done. Let me know if anyone gets in your way or otherwise hinders your efforts. Also, I want a totally new maintenance crew assigned, that includes officers; I'll handle the brass. One more thing, you and the General of the Air Force, be at my office at two o'clock tomorrow afternoon. I'm going to spend the next seven hours with family and try to relax; lift off is set for 1800."

Finally, we land in the homeland; how I miss this place. I see David is here to meet me.

"Hi David, where's Elizabeth and the children?"

"Pop they're at home; the Secret Service thought it best if they stayed there."

"Is there a problem?" "No, they just wanted to be extra cautious; at least that's what they said."

"Director Yates, please walk with me."

"For the next few hours, I don't want to be disturbed, unless it's important. I need time alone with the kids, understood."

"Yes sir."

"Hi Elizabeth, hi kids, it's great to be home."

"Mr. President, I need to speak to you."

"What is Yates?" "Sir, I just received word Admiral Timm was shot and killed."

"Do you know what happened?"

"Mr. President, reports say Wayne Roberts shot him then turned the gun on himself."

"Has Washington gone mad?"

"Alert the flight crew, I want to leave as quickly as possible. Kids give me a hug."

"Dad, do you have to go?"

"Yes, Elizabeth I do, I don't have time to explain."
"Goodbye David."

"Bye dad, we love you."

"I love you." "Yates, I want extra security for the Cabinet members and the Speaker of the House."

"Let's go."

If the next few months are anything like the past ten days, there'll be many a sleepless night. Change is a constant, I accept that; although don't always covet it. It's going it alone.

We are now in the air; I can feel trouble already.

"Mr. President, you have an emergency call on the 'hot line'."